RIVER OF DEMENTIA
a memoir

Pauli Pedersen

BLUE FORGE PRESS
Port Orchard, Washington

River of Dementia
Copyright 2021
by Pauli Pedersen

First eBook Edition December 2021
First Print Edition December 2021
Second eBook Edition December 2023
Second Print Edition December 2023

ISBN 978-1-59092-976-6

All rights reserved, including the right to reproduce this book or portions thereof in any form whatsoever, except in the case of short excerpts for use in reviews of the book. For information about film, reprint or other subsidiary rights, contact: blueforgegroup@gmail.com

This book is a memoir. It reflects the authors' present recollections of experiences over time. While all the stories in this book are true as the author remembers them, some names and identifying details may have been changed to protect the privacy of the people involved.

Blue Forge Press is the print division of the volunteer-run, federal 501(c)3 nonprofit company, Blue Forge Group, founded in 1989 and dedicated to bringing light to the shadows and voice to the silence. We strive to empower storytellers across all walks of life with our four divisions: Blue Forge Press, Blue Forge Films, Blue Forge Gaming, and Blue Forge Records. Find out more at www.BlueForgeGroup.org

Blue Forge Press
7419 Ebbert Drive Southeast
Port Orchard, Washington 98367
blueforgepress@gmail.com
360-550-2071 ph.txt

*To Pop and Nana
and their family.*

ACKNOWLEDGEMENTS

I have a village to thank. My husband Morrie journeyed with me editing, brainstorming, and supporting. Elizabeth Murray's classes and friendship showed me the path. My wonderful workshop friends whose encouragement and positive examples helped make my story better: Katrinka Mannelly for her steadfast belief; Cassandra Amouak-Hale; Ken Malich; Loren Aikins; Max Aikins; Dave Martyn for showing the way; Pat Lowenger; and Dennis Percy.

My grown children helped me remember: Jennifer Ivester; Jeff Pedersen; Chris Pedersen; Amie Carr; Anika Dubois. Sisters Alice Jorgensen and Robin Chaloupka, cousins Jean Stewart, Leonard Nelson, and Sandi Stewart enriched my story.

My friends, Marie Weis, and Dave and Carolyn Mumper, helped polish my work.

Norma Sax carefully edited my finished transcript, and Brianne DiMarco saw promise in my memoir and accepted it for publishing.

I am deeply grateful.

TABLE OF CONTENTS

	ON REFLECTION OF DEMENTIA	9
1	THE PINE BOX	13
2	ROBERT	17
3	JOHN GILBERT DAVISON	23
4	POP AND NANA	27
5	LIFE ON THE PRAIRIE	35
6	NORTH BEACH	42
7	GRAPEVIEW	51
8	DEARLY BELOVED	55
9	GRANDMA ALICE, INVISIBLE	61
10	LITTLE PAULINE	71
11	YOUNG DAD	81
12	EDMONDS	93
13	WINDOVER FARM	101

14 CHRISTMAS CAROL	*113*
15 ROUGH RAPIDS	*127*
16 CHANGES	*137*
17 MONEY LAUNDERING	*143*
18 ROBERT DITCHES PAULINE	*149*
19 KILLING KATS	*153*
20 MEASURING THE BATHROOM	*158*
21 CLASS REUNION	*165*
22 NO PICNIC	*171*
23 PSYCH 101	*177*
24 PSYCH 102	*185*
25 GONE WITH THE WINDOVER	*191*
26 RESOLUTION	*195*
27 THE END	*203*
EPILOGUE	*209*

On Reflection of Dementia

A little snow-melt trickle winks and twinkles in the sun,
dancing down the packed and piney forest floor.
It skips, childlike, to meet the other trickle children running faster
 on the gentle hill, to jump and splash together, over rocky slopes,
 to merge with becks and brooks and rivulets,
  into a growing stream.

Rushing down the incline with abandon, 'til the descent steepens,
 droplets lose control and fly in air while falling
  into deep and darkening pools.

The pools reflect the blackened sky and rise to overflowing,
as the rain joins in, and splatters mountain slope and sapling, forest,
 flowers and all elements beneath the angry canopy,
and lightning stabs the universe.

The storm abates, and sun streaks through the clouds.
The water shouts with freedom, bounding off cliff's edge,
 leaps into space, lands unified in icy lake.

Floating silently through inlets, armlets, coves and bays,
 typical of flowing bodies yielding to the current's pull,
 tickled by the gilded lake fish, flitting in their emerald home,
the drops, united, move past mudslides, tangled trees, and boulders,
 toward the spillway's beckoning.

The ever-moving water rushes over weir and down the flume,
out to mighty Mother River, moving slowly, toward the coast.
Falls and rapids check the progress, flip and toss, creating chaos.
Roiling loss, confusion, follow, as the river rolls along.

Finally surf of salty ocean meets the coursing surge downstream,
 and the single little droplet vanishes in open sea.

RIVER OF DEMENTIA

a memoir

Pauli Pedersen

CHAPTER ONE
The Pine Box
August 1996

My dad's father, almost 103 when he died, didn't want a funeral. He joked about being put in a cardboard box and thrown into a gully without any fuss.

Dad just wanted a pine box.

His favorite woodworking shop in Yakima was the perfect place to fashion his special coffin. Mom's loving order is now ready. My sisters Alice and Robin, Mom, and I are traveling to eastern Washington to pick it up. We can use this break. Dad's illness has been a heavy load. The knockout count started even earlier than we thought. However Alice, Robin, and I have carried weight before, learning to fight gravity when our sister Carol was dying of cervical cancer. We shared the burden with Mom and Dad then. Mom was so overwhelmed, we thought she had Alzheimer's. She didn't.

We call ourselves "the four-headed hydra," a metaphor for our relationship; each of us brings a specific talent to deal with the complex whole. Mom brings optimism and boundless energy. Alice is a mover and shaker. She doesn't take no for an answer. Robin is the hunter-gatherer who quietly takes care of our needs. I bring strength. I'm able to "walk through the valley of the shadow of death" with those I love. We work well together.

As Robin's van pulls up to the Apple Tree Lodge, the empty parking lot radiates heat waves from the blacktop. Built between the freeway and a bend in the Yakima River, the Lodge is a pleasant place to stay. We get out, stretch in the late afternoon sun, and enter the quiet lobby where a bowl of shiny red apples welcomes us at the reception desk. After registering, we head for our air-conditioned room, glad for this time together to grant Dad's funeral wish. Our room is neat, clean, and nearly new. Out the window, across the parking lot, the red, fluorescent Kmart sign captures our attention. That would be a good place to find a tarp to hide the conspicuous coffin, which will be secured to the top of the van on the trip home.

The smell of popcorn draws us from the sweltering heat through the automatic doors, into lovely, refrigerated air. On the camping aisle, shelves carry only camouflage tarps. I put one in the basket. The irony of covering Dad's casket with a camo tarp, so opposite his nature, tickles me; it would have tickled him, too. We start for the checkout when bright orange, green, and blue lights flashing from multiple screens in the electronics department catch Mom's thrifty eye.

"Look. Those TVs are on sale," Mom says. "Wow, it's really a good deal. Could you fit one in your van if I bought it, Robin?" I feel that ironic tickle again.

"Sure Mom," Robin says.

We push our cart past the women's department. "See those purses? They're discounted and I've been looking for a new one. Do you mind if we stop?" Mom asks.

Misery has no shelf life in our family; we mostly revert to humor. The incongruity of a shopping spree during our funeral errand is absurd. But, that's Mom, a sweet and frugal spirit, packaged in a tireless and positive personality, delighted with her treasures and the money she saved. She echoes Pollyanna, though her name is Pauline.

The next morning's bright sun, sneaking through a crack in the dark curtains, wakes us early. We dress, deciding a short stroll along the riverwalk this shiny August morning would be an uplifting way to start our day. Mom's chronic backache keeps her from going, but my sisters and I laugh and talk as we amble toward the sparkling river at the bottom of the hill, on the paved trail between the freeway on-ramp and the hotel. Happy birdsong and sage-filled morning air—cool and refreshing, not yet scorched—ease our ragged spirits as the water sweeps peacefully away. Suddenly, the calm is jarred by a shout.

"Hey, you fat grandma bitches!" yells a man, his rusty yellow car speeding down the on-ramp onto the freeway. We look behind us to see at whom he is yelling. There's no one there. He's hollering at *us*! Three good-natured, rotund, and ripening ladies, out for a walk, a day before our father's funeral. It's awful—and darkly funny. A great name for a music group. "Come hear the *"Fat Grandma Bitches,"* Sunday at the Bay Vista Nursing Home."

In spite of our strange morning, we pulled up to the carpentry shop at seven thirty a.m. The pine box is beautiful, fragrant of fresh-cut wood—long smooth boards of light saffron and cream, striated with golden streaks, topped by a lid that fits perfectly without a wiggle. A craftsman ties the empty box securely to the top of Robin's minivan, adjusts the camo tarp, and we are on the road to Seattle by eight o'clock a.m. The highway flows through leafy apple orchards, desert hills, the hay-making Kittitas Valley, then the foothill city of Cle Elum where we stop at McKeans's Drive-In for our favorite giant burgers. As we continue up through the Cascade Mountains to Snoqualmie Pass, then downhill to Seattle, the camo tarp does nothing to disguise the coffin on the top of the van.

We deliver the pine box to the Evergreen Washelli Funeral Home and the new TV to Mom's house. Our pilgrimage-cum-shopping spree is done. A bittersweet journey, comforting, because we fulfilled Dad's wish.

CHAPTER TWO
Robert
1917

Through the golden glow of the past, I see a small boy running across an open prairie, his dog Bonus at his side, free and wild in the morning heat, over the fields of gestating wheat, full of the promise of growing up at the beginning of a new century. During the first five years of his life, the First World War burned away, the Titanic and the Lusitania sank, and Mata Hari was shot as a spy, while Robert played happily on the Montana homestead, untouched by the world's chaos. This is the life story of my Dad.

I grew up with the tale of Dad's days on the homestead lilting through my childhood like a melody. A melody of reminiscence, longing, and the romance of the old west. The Davison family remembered the time on the ranch lovingly, sharing only the best stories—not the sub-zero winters, scorching summers, spring plowing in knee-deep mud, flies, rattlesnakes, or hard scrabble living. As an adult, Dad felt he'd lived the perfect boyhood, though it was

18   *River of Dementia*

only five years, on the homestead in Carter, Montana.

"It's a boy," announced the nurse, swaddling the squirming newborn into a warm bundle and nestling him in his mother's arms. "This isn't like the others, Mrs. Davison," the doctor said as he untied his surgical apron. "This little one is healthy and should be fine. We'll watch you both over the next couple of weeks and then you can go home. Will you have help there?"

"I will, Dr Olson. My oldest girls are almost grown. They'll be able to see after everything 'til I'm up and around."

"That's good. Now, I'll go and tell your husband that he has a new son!" He bowed courteously and walked toward the door. "Don't forget to have the baby registered at the courthouse," he advised, "sooner rather than later."

My father, Robert Edward Davison, was born on a

Christel, Letha, Paul, Queena, Phyllis and Baby Robert

windy day of 1912, March 12, in the Columbus Hospital of Great Falls, Montana. His parents, Philip and Ivy Davison—to me they were Pop and Nana—had moved their family from Pennsylvania in 1909. Robert was welcomed, later, as the youngest of six children, joining his brother Paul, next youngest, and four sisters: Christel, Phyllis, Letha, and Queena, youngest to oldest.

    His oldest sister, Queena Wanima, conjured an Indian princess. The family called her "Queenie," although she preferred the more modern "Juanita." When Dad was born, she was sixteen and teaching school in the grassland town of Geraldine, outside of Fort Benton, Montana. Every school day at dawn her lithe figure could be seen riding a bay horse into the sunrise and across the prairie to her one-room schoolhouse. She would stoke the fire in the stove, sweep and dust the room, clean the chalkboard and straighten the desks and chairs before the children arrived. At noon, while the schoolchildren walked home for lunch, she would feed grain to her horse—Queenie had two she'd alternate, Buck and Beau—and eat the lunch she had brought from home, which could include a stew from last night, or a biscuit and beans. If she were lucky, she might find one of her sister Letha's tasty molasses cookies. All day long she would encourage young minds like a sculptor shaping clay. At the end of the school day, she would correct slates, tidy her books and ride home in the fall heat or winter snow. She married a Montanan who fought in World War I but divorced him when his drinking and fists got the best of him. She became a poet after raising her boys as a single parent. Intelligent and gracious, she was my first example of an "independent woman."

Queenie Davison (center, back) and her students in Geraldine, Montana

Ride, old Buck, wherever you are,
Over a grateful plain;
Ride the night from star to star,
Wind upon your mane...
Ride as we used to long ago,
Trails to far off skies;
Tang of sage on melting snow,
While a winter dies...

From the book of poems *Singing Down The Dawn*, by Queena Davison Miller. I have always been proud of her sylvan artistry.

Letha, thirteen, Dad's second oldest sister, put a button up her nose as a toddler. The resulting infection turned into spinal meningitis. She survived, but her fragile heart led to a life of doctor visits. She never married, but lived at home to take care of her mother, and her doctors became her beaus. She loved us nieces and spoiled us with treats and loving attention.

Phyllis, ten, had dark hair, and Christel, seven, had light. They were pretty little girls, who learned to sew, and clean, do the washing and ironing, and preserve food for winter, all the uxorial arts their older sisters had learned from their mama. They grew into beautiful women and beloved aunties who pampered my sisters and me as Robert's little girls.

Paul, five, was full of pepper. Whenever devilry was afoot, it ran with Paul. Chasing the baby calves, jumping from the chicken house into the pigsty, painting his face black with chimney soot to scare his sisters, he was a whirling dervish as he grew. A mischief-maker like his father, when he finished high school, he headed for California where he married and raised his family.

Dad had his mother's personality—sweet, gentle, and shy, the opposite of his prankish older brother. Nana's provincial nature, with a distrust of "interlopers," and fear of cards and dancing, undoubtedly affected Dad's overly cautious nature. He spent his life tending a "worry gene" that grew until it swallowed him.

A winsome child with fine brown hair and even features, his boyishly handsome face still peaked from his salt and pepper hair when he died at 84. As a young man, he was small and slight like Charlie Chaplin. He loved Charlie Chaplin. Dad's green eyes sprouted laugh lines with Chaplin's antics and deepened as he encountered more of life's merrymaking. When Dad laughed hard, his eyes squeezed shut and tearing up, he'd whoop the laughter out. It was the soundtrack of our childhood. He loved jokes and used his whimsical sense of humor as lessons.

About tact: *"What would be better to say?"* he'd ask. *"Your face could stop a clock, or when I saw you, time* stood still?"

About choice: *Never wrestle with a pig. You both get dirty and the pig likes it.* This and other advice I use today.

My sisters remember his joke:

Father:"Yittle Yobby, yump to your Pappa."
Boy:"No, Pappa, I don't want to yump."
Father: "Yittle Yobby, your Pappa will catch you."
Boy: "No Pappa, I'm afraid."
Father: "Don't worry Yittle Yobby, I will catch you."
Boy:"But Pappa..."
Father: "Yump, Yittle Yobby. Yump!"
So Yittle Yobby yumped and fell splat on the floor.
Boy: "Pappa," he cried, "you said you would catch me."
Father: "Let this be a lesson, my son. Never trust anyone, not even your pappa."

Dad found this very funny. I think it was the subtext of his life. He was the baby of the family but as he grew up his father's unreliability subtly shifted family responsibilities onto Dad like a drip slowly filling a bucket.

My grandmother carried the weight of stability for the family and Dad helped her until he could take it over. In high school, he added his paper route money to his sisters' salaries to help their mama pay the mortgage. After graduating from high school he gave his mama most of his salary while working for a shop that sold window shades. At 24 he opened his own business and continued supporting his mother's small lifestyle, as well as providing jobs for his two sisters, one divorced and one unmarried. Unlike his father, who was 47 when Dad was born, he was as dependable as Greenwich Mean Time.

CHAPTER THREE
John Gilbert Davison
1912

My grandfather, "Pop," was a rascal. His Scottish heritage provided his stubbornness and his Irish ancestors gave him the twinkle in his eye. He was generally a good man but did as he pleased throughout his long life. And it was a long life—six months short of his 103rd birthday. He was a hard worker with a playful spirit who left the responsibilities of life to others.

I was too young to understand any of this, except to identify with his playful spirit naturally recognized by a child. He was pal, protector, and refuge from hard knocks like the birth of my new baby sister. When I was a toddler, he was my hero.

His six children grew up learning that to depend on him was fruitless and turned to help their mom meet the family crises—the Great Depression being one—and make good lives for themselves.

Even acknowledging his care-free attitude, no one could have imagined the family secret he kept for 46 years.

Maybe he forgot, or maybe he was just waiting for the fun of discovery.

Several days after my dad was born, it was time to name and register the new baby. Nana, from the large, Scots-Irish Gahagan family, was certain about the names she wanted, Robert and Edward, after "the two famous kings who fought for Scotland," she said. Robert the Bruce had won Scottish independence from England's Edward the First.

Resting in the hospital, Nana sent Pop to the Great Falls Courthouse to register their new baby boy, Robert Edward Davison. But, my grandfather, impulsive as well as mischievous, preferred the names John and Gilbert, after his two favorite brothers, one older than he, and the other younger. So, instead, he registered the baby as John Gilbert Davison, then failed to mention it to anyone.

For over 40 years Dad lived with the name Robert Edward Davison. As a baby, he was nicknamed Yittle Yobbie (Little Robert), and as a child, he was always called Robert Edward. He signed his marriage license in that name, incorporated his business under that name, signed the birth certificates of his four daughters, took out his driver's licenses, and signed his business checks with that name.

In 1960, after winning a business contest for a trip to Spain, he went to apply for a passport and found there was no record of a Robert Edward Davison born in Montana on March 12, 1912. There was a John Gilbert Davison born on the same day at the same time. I can imagine Dad shaking his head when he realized who was responsible. Nana knew nothing about this, but when the spotlight fell on my grandfather, his rascally grin gave him away. Nana had been putting up with his tomfoolery for years, and legally corrected his mischief. After 46 years, Dad was finally legal and able to spend a wonderful week in southern Spain. My grandfather was 93 when this shenanigan came to light.

Later, when Dad became someone else, we called him John—the man no one knew existed.

CHAPTER FOUR
Pop and Nana
1890s

The small, muscular logger banged his whiskey glass on the bar and stepped between the two brawlers. "Leave it be!" he bellowed over the noise, "Get your G.D.... carcasses out the door and leave the drinking to your betters!" He stared, steely-eyed, at the drunken pair. The shorter man, with the stink of manure riding him, hauled back his fist for the first punch when his quicker, tobacco squirting cohort caught the logger with a swift blow to his cheek. The fight grew as friends from both sides were drawn into the melee. The logger ducked a blow and as he stood up was cracked under his left eye. His vision blurred and as he reached to his eye, found his eyeball hanging out of its socket next to his nose. With the top of his right forefinger, he slurped it back into its socket and continued the fight.

This was my grandfather, my father's father, my gateway to the past as far back as the Great Civil War. Philip Sheridan Davison—my dad called him Pop—was born in Pennsylvania on November 27, 1865, seven months after the assassination of Abraham Lincoln. He was proudly named after the Union General, Philip Henry Sheridan, who "electrified the North in 1864 by destroying the Confederate South's food supply in the Shenandoah Valley."

His family's Scots roots were planted in Massachusetts after exile by Cromwell's Parliament for taking part in the Covenanter's Resistance to the English Army in 1650. By the 1800s his family had migrated to Pennsylvania where father, Charles Watson Davison, and mother, Mary Boyd Eckman, were married one month before the Civil War began.

Pop was the third of eight children and born a scalawag. He loved his brothers, John and Gilbert, his cohorts in mayhem. He disliked his older sister, Elizabeth, because she was aloof and teased him with "Sherry-Dan, Sherry-Dan," a nickname he hated.

Phillip Sheridan Davison ("Pop")

His revenge was petty. When both were teens, he invited her to a party in town and when she was dressed in her fancy dress, waiting on the porch, he drove his buggy up and passed her as he continued into town without stopping.

That amused him. He knew how to step on sore toes.

Pop grew up with his grandfather living with the family, as my sisters and I did. His grandfather, "old Coddington," he called him, had a "terrible movement of body." It's intriguing to imagine what that meant. It may have been related to the lifelong tic that troubled my father's brother, Paul. Pop's family of thirteen children lived a hardscrabble life. His father, Charles, wounded in the Civil War, could not provide well for his family. At one point the children were parceled out to relatives to help the family survive. Young Philip was sent to live with an uncle. They ate a lot of buttermilk-soaked bread with brown sugar he said, as his uncle had little to share.

As a young man, Philip was a dandy with wavy brown hair cut short and combed to the right. He was clean-shaven but sported a medium-sized mustache and sky-blue eyes. At 18, he met Miram Deemer—it was spelled Miram on their 1885 marriage license, though other sources have mistaken it for Miriam—a petite brown-haired beauty. He told me "her nostrils were so close together she had to pick her nose with a pin!" They married in 1883 and had a daughter they named Anna Pearl in April of 1887. That fall, Pop and Miram contracted typhoid fever and Miram died on Christmas Day. Pop was so ill, he didn't know his wife died until after she was buried. Pearl was eight months old. Too young to stay with her father.

Anna Pearl Davison

He returned to the woods, a widower, and Pearl went to live with her Deemer grandparents, who worried that her father might take her away. Pearl remained close to her grandmother, Mary Davison, but sadly, never saw her father again after he left Pennsylvania when she was twelve. It seems very unfair that my sisters and I enjoyed the close connection with our grandfather that his daughter, Pearl, never had.

We little girls loved Pop's stories, watching him, wide-eyed, as he'd regale us with his scary tale. My favorite began:

I was fifteen feet up on the staging of a great cedar tree, working one end of a cross-cut saw, sawdust flying in my eyes at each swoosh of a big cut. Suddenly, I heard a terrifying scream below. I scrambled down to the ground where a man, on his knees, was looking down, dumbfounded, at the double blade axe sticking out of his chest. He'd tripped and fallen. White with shock, he started to pull at the handle. STOOOOP!! I hollered. The blade came out and blood gushed everywhere. I tugged the man to his feet, reached into his chest and clamped my hand around the spurting artery. Holding it together, we ran for camp, over wood chips and tangled branches, trying to keep our balance, huffing in the smell of blood and pine. When we reached the doctor's tent, they had to pry my fingers loose.

It was an exciting story for little girls. I never asked about what became of the man; I was fixated on Pop's hand squeezing the bloody artery. I doubt the man survived, since his wound was so severe, and little was known about sepsis. Our grandfather was a grand spinner of tales.

The Gahagan household was a bees' nest of activity with thirteen children, counting half-brothers and sisters. As the twelfth child of Almanda Howard and Charles McDonald Gahagan, my grandmother, Iva Ersa—Nana—born in 1877 Pennsylvania, grew into a lithe and capable girl with chestnut hair, blue eyes, and a serious nature. The 1892 household was crowded and spare, so in exchange for room and board, Nana at 15, and her sister Jenny, 16, went to work in the boarding house of their Uncle Sherm's logging camp for room and board. Her Presbyterian upbringing taught her the dangers of dancing and card playing, but for all her seriousness, she always enjoyed a good beer and a good chuckle. That is probably why she was attracted to the

Iva Ersa Gahagan

slight, clean-shaven logger with bright blue eyes, who would tease her at dinner times. He would hide the salt shaker and ask her for more salt or pretend to drop a bowl that would cause her to jump for it and then he would grin with merriment in his eyes. They married in Pennsylvania in 1896. He was eleven years her senior.

Their early years of marriage were spent in Indiana County, Pennsylvania, in the same township where parents, grandparents, brothers, and sisters lived. Pop continued logging and Nana had the children. Queenie came first, then Letha, Phyllis, Christel, and Paul followed in 1907.

The Indian wars in Montana had been over for twenty-seven years, when the Enlarged Homestead Act of 1909 doubled the 160 acres of free land to 320 acres, and the railroads began filling Montana with more settlers and businesses to serve the growing population. Pop's brothers, John and Gilbert, and his sister, Estella, had migrated to Montana. When Pop proposed the idea, Nana must have agreed to go, though it meant leaving all that was familiar to her. On the other hand, as one of thirteen children, she may have looked forward to the breathing space of a fresh situation.

Following John, Gilbert, and Estella, Pop and his family left Pennsylvania in May of 1909, for the small town of Carter, Montana, outside of Great Falls.

Carter and towns like it were developed by the Great Northern Railroad to expand business. By shipping machinery and dry goods, providing fast transportation, and exporting agricultural products like wheat and cattle from the new markets, the railroad increased its profits.

Pop's land lay near his siblings. On a sunny day in

spring, he carefully selected the placement of their home with a creek nearby, unaware that in the summer the creek dried up and the walk to water was a half-mile. In winter, water was right outside the door in the form of five-foot drifts of snow. Undaunted, Letha learned how to make snow ice cream by mixing a tub of the crunchy crystals with evaporated milk, sugar and vanilla to make their favorite winter dessert.

Even enabled by the railroads, the Davison family's trip across the United States from Pennsylvania to Montana took three days.

CHAPTER FIVE
Life on the Prairie
1909-1920

The train whistle screamed at the Pittsburgh, Pennsylvania train station, declaring departure. The year was 1909 and the train carried my grandparents, and their five children on the journey to Carter, Montana, and 320 acres of free farmland. Pop filed the paperwork, paid the $18 fee under The Enlarged Homestead Act of February 1909, and began the adventure to better his life by improving his land for the five years required to secure the deed. This is my heritage, gained from Dad's family—a front-row seat to the romance of life in the old west.

Imagine the relief, joy, and terror in their hearts as the train pulled from the station and their new life began.

"Hurry up Phyllis, the train will be moving any minute."

"I can't find my doll," she whined. "Mama! I can't find my Lucy!"

"Hush," Queenie, the eldest at twelve, continued,

"Mama's busy with little Paul. Just get into your seat and we'll find your Lucy later." Phyllis, seven, began to cry. Little Christel, six, on the seat opposite began to sniffle in sympathy. "Now, now sweet girls, stop your crying and I'll tell you a story," 10-year-old Letha crooned. She stood on tiptoes to shove her reticule onto the shelf above, lowered herself into the seat next to Phyllis, and began, "Once upon a time...."

Three days later, a mighty locomotive pulled up to the Carter depot. Seven very weary Davisons exited the cramped train car. Parents stretched while children ran. Within the hour, wagons arrived, and the station filled with happy relatives. The wagons were loaded up with crates and trunks, and they all headed to Gilbert's place where Pop's family would stay temporarily.

After resting several days, the Davison brothers, Estella's husband, neighbors, and younger cousins banded together for a barn raising. The next week the house was started, and with all the hands to help, it wasn't long before the four-room soddie was ready. Nana and the family moved in and Pop took the train to Glacier National Park to begin his job building structures for the Parks Department.

Their house was close enough to Carter to keep their coal bucket filled for cooking and heating, and to make it easy to take the train into Great Falls for appointments or fun. Christel, Dad's youngest sister, remembered displaced Indian men hanging around the Carter train station, in boredom, watching the passengers come and go. When she was little, walking by the scowling faces each time she took the train to Great Falls made her uncomfortable.

Because Pop was an experienced logger from the forests

Deed to Davison Homestead

of Pennsylvania, working as a logger in the western wilderness provided money for homestead improvements. But, he had to spend springs and summers away from home, while Nana, and Pop's brothers and cousins shared the plowing, planting, harvesting, and farm work needing to be done. He had signed on with a company constructing government buildings in Glacier National Park and worked building barracks, workshops, cabins, and lodges, including the East Glacier Lodge where, he would tell me, giant trees held up the second and third story balconies.

The family had lived in Montana for three years when Robert was born. After two miscarriages, he was a special treasure. As soon as he was able, he roamed the prairie. For five years he knew nothing else. This cherished beginning glowed within him the rest of his life.

"Robert! Paul! Get down off that consarned roof!" The whip snapped close to Robert's four-year-old leg. *The boys scrambled quickly to the ground and stood sheepishly before their mama as the prairie breeze ruffled their blond hair. "You know I've told you to stay off there! Now, go draw water from the cistern. The buckets are in the house, and if I catch you up there again, I'll use this on you for sure!" She nodded to the whip in her hand.*

From a distance, the house looked like part of the low hills rising above a vast prairie. Their home was called a "soddie." Other settlers had built their soddies completely with the earthen bricks cut from the tight, intricate root systems of the dense prairie grasses. But Pop used lumber to build three walls into the hillside, then covered his wood ceiling with prairie sod. That way the insects, vermin, and dirt rarely fell from above, like they did in other homes built with a netting of twigs, small branches, and hay to hold up the sod. Pop then used sod against the wooden outside walls, insulating them from wind and snow in the

Davison children and cousins, 1916

winter or stifling heat in the summer. When finished, the house looked like a cozy animal shelter.

Nana raised six children in the four-room home. She carried water from the creek a half-mile away, or the nearby cistern when the rains were good. The outhouse was fifty steps toward the chicken coop. She made and washed clothes, parceled out food supplies, cared for the animals, maintained the buildings, planted and cultivated the garden in the spring, canned and preserved vegetables through the summer and fall. Through wicked summer heat and bitter winter snows, for the required five years, she managed the homestead and five, then six children, during the time Pop was working in Glacier National Park. There was always a storm of playmates around, with the myriad of cousins and friends who lived in the area.

It's hard for each generation to see the significance of their ordinary life, but the past carries lessons and treasures for those who want to mine. When I was old enough in the 1960s to dig into Nana's prairie adventures, she was far past those hard years, worn out and reserved. The stories about homesteading came mostly from my Auntie Letha, who spent her life taking care of Nana, or from Auntie Queenie, the oldest child in the family, or from my dad, who longed to return to those halcyon years. Nana lived to be 86 and died in the spring of 1963, just missing the assassination of JFK, which was the fourth presidential assassination since her birth in 1877.

"It's Dad! Dad's coming," they shouted when they saw the bulging wagon coming down the road from town, pulled by two strong horses. "He's got presents! I know he's got presents!" The horses ambled into the yard, and Pop jumped down from the wagon seat.

"Here, horehound for everyone!" He grinned as he shoved the candy sticks into eager hands. The older girls stood back, waiting their turns. He loved the ruckus of coming home from the logging camp. Nana stood in the shade of the hut's doorway.

They unloaded everything from the heaped-up wagon: heavy sacks of flour and sugar, cornmeal, a barrel of molasses, several sides of bacon, salt, tea, vinegar, soda, lard wrapped in wax-paper packages, twine, needles, tools, a couple of books, newspapers. Things to last for three months or more, until time to come back again with more supplies from his wages.

"Here, Ivy, I brought you coffee," he chuckled, extending the small package which she took with a smile.

"I knew you'd be here soon bein' as the flour and lard have about run out." She put the precious package in the pie safe for later. "Virgil's plowed our 100 acres, so you

can help with the planting tomorrow. How long are you staying?"

"I can take two days. That's enough to help with the plantin', then I'll be headin' back."

"Well, supper's ready. Go call the children."

By 1914 the homestead was a working ranch, the deed was earned, and Pop was 51. The family stayed on for a few more years, but he was a restless soul looking for more out of life. He sold the ranch and moved his family into a modest house in Great Falls around 1918. Compared to the soddie, it seemed a castle.

The younger girls enrolled in high school and the boys, elementary school. School was new to Robert, but he took to it. However, he suffered painful headaches some days, and had to lie in the dark for hours with wet cloths on his forehead. When the doctor first gave him aspirin and his headaches went away, he became a devotee to the power of medicine.

Not long after they moved, six-year-old Robert woke from a deep sleep to pandemonium outside. Church bells were ringing, whistles shrieking, guns firing, a great clamor sounding. It was midnight. Parents and siblings crept to the windows, to see what was causing the commotion. Lights were coming on in other houses in their new neighborhood. Pop went for his gun, then eased the front door open a crack to peek into the night. The noise grew louder. It was November 11, 1918. The Germans had surrendered, The Great War was over, and the people of Great Falls were celebrating.

Queenie, who had been teaching in Great Falls, married her handsome soldier at the end of the Great War, and welcomed baby Wally in 1919.

The Davison family spent two school years in town, and then Pop decided to move to Seattle. Why did they all move to Seattle? Maybe it was the Chamber of Commerce's national ad campaign in 1919—"Seattle Invites you to a Charmed Land"—that brought them there.

CHAPTER SIX
North Beach
1920—1938

Seattle was bustling when Pop's family arrived from Montana in the summer of 1920. The Roaring Twenties were the same in Seattle as most of the United States. Prohibition hung over the city and although there were temperance lobbyists and suffragists, flappers, bootleggers, and speakeasies were tucked away in the surrounding Puget Sound area. The Alaskan gold rush was coming to an end after fourteen years. Bill Boeing's company was four years old, as were the Ballard Locks.

The family rented a house on Phinney Ridge above Ballard, and below Woodland Park Zoo. Pop's brother Gilbert followed with his family, and the brothers found work as carpenters. Pop called Gilbert "Pete" and Gilbert called Pop "Joe" for their own amusement. The family's embarrassing secret was that Uncle Pete liked to wear women's silk panties—to keep from chafing, he said.

They arrived between wars, when the city life was

generally calm before the next storms hit. Ignorant of the open segregation shown on maps of the time and the union unrest lingering after the Seattle General Strike the year before, the family settled in without much fuss. Queenie, Joe, and Wally settled nearby, with another baby on the way.

Pop and his brother began their acquaintance with Seattle, gambling at night on the busy waterfront. One evening, a stranger sidled up to them.

"*Say, fellas, know anyone who'd be interested in making a bit of money? I've got something here that will make some young buck a rich man. Wish I could use it, but I'm headed for the Alaska gold fields.*"

"*What're you talkin' about?*" Pete asked.

That evening, Pop brought home a $500 secret doughnut recipe, paid for from the $8000 he'd gotten for selling the homestead. Through his rose-colored glasses, Pop imagined the doughnut's secret formula would make him a rich man. He took his 12-year-old son Paul, traveled three hours south to Portland, Oregon, rented a space, purchased equipment, and opened a doughnut shop. The doughnuts were delicious, tasting of cinnamon and mace. Mace, the hidden ingredient, is similar to nutmeg but comes from the outside hull of the nutmeg kernel. The aroma was heavenly.

"Come and get your fresh, hot doughnuts here!" Paul would shout out to the people walking by. "Get your baker's dozen doughnuts, fresh today!"

Customers came and went, but never enough to cover expenses. After several disappointing months, Pop and Paul came home, heads hung low. With Pop, shenanigans were always within reach. Nana stoically persevered.

Though work as a carpenter made a fair wage, Pop's appetite for "visiting the Chinamen," a euphemism for waterfront gambling, made him an unreliable source of income. The family, however, eked by. Pop occasionally found his "sweet spot," but lost more than he won, so Nana, like most mothers, had long been able to spin straw into gold.

Little white houses, across the railroad tracks from a sandy beach, make a cheerful setting for the small Seattle community of North Beach. Robert was in the seventh grade when Pop found a small, two-bedroom, gable-roofed house there, two blocks from the seashore. Fishing, swimming, sunbathing, and sea life lay before them. Pop made the down payment. They left Phinney Ridge and moved twenty minutes to the north. Nana paid the monthly mortgage, with help from Robert's paper route money and

Little White House at North Beach

his sisters' jobs at Woolworths and Rhodes. Pop, Nana, Robert, and Letha lived in the new little house; Queenie lived nearby with her two boys; Phyllis and Christel were married with their own homes, and Paul had moved to California. Over the years, Nana would cross the tracks with a grandchild or two, climb down the riprap to the sand, and hunt for oysters at low tide. When she found one, she would whip a small knife from the pocket of her long, dark skirt, pry the bivalve open, and slurp the salty treat from the shell to the surprise of her young companions. She was comfortable in her little home by the beach, even after Pop moved in with us, and filled her days with leisure and detective magazines she hid under the sofa. She passed away in 1963, at age 86.

To my youthful eyes, the little white house near the beach was a sanctuary, shady and peaceful. An ancient blooming Christmas cactus sat by the front door. Light from four, tall rectangular windows filtered by lacy white curtains, spread through the small living room, nurturing the venerable old plant. The L-shaped room held a comfy sofa at

Robert Davison, 12

the long end and an old-fashioned dining table of dark wood, covered with a hand-made lace tablecloth, at the other.

The scent of roses always filled the room of my memories; leafy, red and yellow petaled blooms on the dining room table arose from an antique vase which repeated their natural beauty with a large dark-red English rose painted on the china surface.

When spending the night, I'd climb the staircase that led to a haven of knotty pine. Nana's room was on the left and Letha's, on the right, always smelled of Faberge's, "Tabeau," the perfume she favored. I slept in Nana's room in a narrow bed under the sloping roof, unmindful of her petite snores. For many years I spent loving times in the little white house, lucky to know the deep bond of family.

At age 62, Pop was still active and full of energy. Somehow, he acquired real estate called Cathcart. Did he win or buy the property? It's hard to know, but the five acres and rude log cabin, northeast of Seattle, appealed to his rustic background, and it became a family gathering place from the late 1920s through the 1930s. Pop and other relatives worked weekends and summers to make the cabin livable, and Robert, 15 by then, labored alongside the others, felling trees, chopping wood for the stove, sharpening his carpentry skills. Queenie and Phyllis would visit with their families, enjoying the picnics Nana and Letha would pack of ham sandwiches, pickled beets, carrot sticks, Letha's molasses cookies, apples from their tree, a thermos of coffee, while their city children ran wild in the woods. Sometimes they all stayed the weekend. Dad's love of getaways and picnics grew from there as "Cathcart" became a special retreat from city life. But when the chance to vacation at Grapeview came along, Pop sold Cathcart.

The year 1928 was memorable. The streetlights of Seattle, five round bulbs in the shape of a triangle, were installed and electrified, and Robert turned 16, unexpectedly getting his first car. One day, Pop brought home a Model T Ford. Maybe because of his diminutive size or Scots inheritance, Pop was always quite sure of himself. He'd been a cheeky young man, and the trait followed him into adulthood. With no license or instruction, he figured it would be as easy to drive a car as a team of horses. He forgot about gravity. At the top of a long, wooded hill that wound down to North Beach, he drew out the choke under the radiator, grabbed the crank, and yanked it to the right with a mighty heave. The engine turned over, and after Pop adjusted the spark lever on the steering column, it purred encouragingly. He hopped in, and with a crooked

Robert Davison, 24 with nephew Wally Miller, 17

smile, pulled the stick on his right, and stomped on the first of three floor pedals. The Model T leaped backwards. He stamped on another pedal and the car halted. The third pedal moved him slowly forward, and the men standing around to watch gave him a push. The tires began to roll, gradually at first, but as the coupe gathered speed, Pop searched for a brake. Where the hell was the brake?! He pulled levers and punched pedals wildly, but the car had gathered too much speed on the steep incline, and nothing worked. White knuckles clenching the steering wheel, heart pounding, he careened down the hill, out of control, spun around a corner, and ran into a neighbor's bush. Silence. Leaping out, shaking, and as pale as goose feathers, Pop handed Robert the keys, and Robert became his chauffeur from then on. In his 103 years of life, Pop never did learn to drive.

The stock market crashed hard the autumn Robert graduated from high school. He was lucky to find a job in a window shade shop where his boss taught him about business. The Great Depression years were lean as he learned his craft. I remember the big ball of rubber bands in Nana's basement, as well as a bigger ball of string. I remember the stashes of waxed paper bread wrappers, and white oleo mixed with yellow coloring to make margarine—all remnants of the Great Depression. A penny saved was a penny earned.

But the most wonderful thing during those troubling years was the weekend trips to Grapeview. Letha's romance brought about a lovely turn of events.

CHAPTER SEVEN
Grapeview
1930—1987

Grapeview became a very special place for the Davison family in the 1930s—twenty-seven acres of woods on a small Puget Sound inlet where a big open clearing contained a cabin, barn and vineyard, and a wide path to the beach. Auntie Letha's English boyfriend, Don McDonald, generously offered it to Letha's family to enjoy. Pop and Nana's family loved Grapeview and its country nature. For years before Dad was married, the family picnicked there, stayed overnight in the old cabin, made jellies or juice from the grapes picked from the vineyard, and enjoyed the beach.

When World War II came, Don McDonald joined the British Armed Forces. He'd been part of the family happiness at Grapeview for a long time, so he transferred the property to Dad, Letha's brother, in the form of a quitclaim deed, in case Don didn't return. I was two when Dad went to work at the nearby Bremerton Navy Yard as a ship painter in the war effort, and Grapeview became a handy place to live for a summer.

A beautiful, wide, tree-canopied lane beside a small creek led downhill to the oystered beach. It was created by the footsteps of men coming up to the cabin when it was a post office for the "Mosquito Fleet," a swarm of small steamers delivering mail and cargo to waterfront sites on Puget Sound, too hard to reach by land. The fleet began after World War I and ceased before our family came, leaving the specter of the past in the leafy shadows of the lane.

Grey weathered boards covered the cabin tucked into the undergrowth, and in the spring wild daffodils, bright yellow with a delicious scent, filled the little dell on the left side. But the old house was scary for a kid. Bats sometimes flew through its two bedrooms, and there were always mice and spiders when we arrived. In a few days, it would be cleaned and warmed by the woodstove into a cozy nest.

Davison Family at Grapeview, 1931

The house was furnished with old, mismatched dishes, silverware, pots and pans, things that would be an antique dealer's dream now, especially the wooden ice box we'd fill with blocks of ice from the country store. There was a double bed in each of the two bedrooms. An overstuffed, brown sofa, blanket-covered daybed, rocking chair with a thick, paisley pillow on the seat, several straight chairs, and a big, round, oak table crowded the small living room. A hand-cranked Victrola sat in the corner in the early years, near a big mahogany, console radio, where we'd gather around eagerly listening to presidential conventions, to find out who would be the new candidate.

Estes Kefauver, a senator from Tennessee, ran as a Democratic presidential nominee in 1952. His theme song was "Davy Crockett," and he was my choice because he gave away "coonskin" hats I coveted. He didn't win the nomination, but the convention was riveting, and as his popularity grew and waned, we sat spellbound around the big cabinet radio, in the peaceful backwoods of western Washington.

We had electricity for lights and the radio, but no running water. Our water came from a well dug near the house. Every few years, Dad or Pop would be lowered into it for cleaning and repairs. The top of the well was surrounded by a wooden frame about four feet high. We would reach over for the heavy, wooden bucket tied to a large pulley, drop the bucket until it hit the water, twelve or so feet down, let it fill, and haul it up, hand over hand. We drew water for drinking, washing dishes and clothes, or baths. For baths, we'd heat water on the woodstove, carry it outside to a galvanized tub set in the long grass, and sit washing our parts. We had no yard. Just a field of tall grass beyond the parked cars.

With a dug well, there was no indoor plumbing. Instead, we used an outhouse we called "King Tut," an inside joke referring to its aged and terrible odor. It was dug a respectable distance from the house, managed with lye, and moved every few years when needed.

When we were all there together—wife, children, Nana, Pop, sisters, brothers-in-law, nieces, and nephews, Dad was a happy soul. Each year, as soon as school was out, he'd take us to Grapeview. He'd go back to the city to work during the week and come back on the weekends to revive and play, a portent of his coming and going on the farm when we moved to Kittitas. As always, he took pleasure in providing others with fun.

Dad bought a small aluminum motorboat for sightseeing, and when we were older he made a "wakeboard" to tow behind the boat. Riding it was scary fun. Later, we moved on to water skis. In good weather, we dug geoducks on the muddy beach when the tide was out. My friend Patsy and I would sneak up on a geoduck, its neck stretched out in the sun. I'd pounce and grab the neck while Patsy would slam the clam shovel under it and out would come a leviathan to grind—its meat was too tough to chop—for this night's chowder. We picked blackberries for pies, sunbathed, and made s'mores over beach fires. When it rained, we played card games inside, around the big, round, oak table. Through the years, Grapeview became our heart, beating in a different place, waiting for our return.

CHAPTER EIGHT
Dearly Beloved
1936—1939

In 1936, at age 24, Dad opened his own shop, selling shades, countertops, and floor coverings, and providing jobs for Queenie and Letha. Starting his business in Ballard during the Great Depression took courage, but also foresight because he had the fishing fleet to supply with countertops and flooring, as well as the homes in the area. Davison's, Inc. had been running smoothly, supporting his sisters and parents for less than two years when he noticed Pauline.

Starting his business had taken hard work, and now, with the success, it was time to start a family. He didn't date but left it to God to find him the perfect girl. And He did. One weekend, Robert's sister Queenie invited him to a church singles group, and there was the pretty girl he knew from the window shade supply store. She was small and winsome; her personality bubbled with fun. She had hair as dark and shiny as black onyx, and eyes deep blue and dazzling. Robert was smitten. Pauline Theda also

Robert in his first Shop 1936

recognized him. In her search for a soul mate, she would soon find that he was the answer to her own prayers. Their life together bloomed from that church social and flowered for 56 years.

My parent's story is a romance. A Cinderella tale. Fair maiden with a wicked stepmother meets handsome, successful bachelor, who sweeps her away to a happy life. An incredibly true beginning, perhaps a balance for the unexpected end.

Dad had a quiet, polite demeanor, and felt more comfortable with simple, unassuming people, and simple, unpretentious ideals. He was wary of worldliness. In later life, we'd watch him stalk out of movies to prove his lofty moral code. Mom was more outgoing and ebullient. In contrast to Dad, she loved socializing and making friends. Together, they shared deep Christian values, which carried them through a life not without hardship. Born in a time of innocence, before the scandalous and sophisticated 1920s, they grew up through the Great Depression era. Dad came from humble beginnings, the prairie and the homestead in Montana, and Mom, genteel indifference. In the future, some family members would mistake their deep-rooted virtue as a lack of experience, and quietly ridicule them as "the Vanilla People."

When Dad proposed, Mom was wise enough to make him wait a year before they married, "so they would know each other better," she said with remarkable restraint. I would have been more inclined to bolt from the Theda household.

The year of engagement was magic: picnics and parties, skiing and dancing, pinochle and church. Time flew through the seasons, and by fall, the wedding date was set for January. They planned and paid for their own wedding, but at the last minute, Pauline's parents decided to contribute ice cream cups to the reception.

As Robert awoke early on his wedding day, a grin spread across his face as he thought of Pauline and their life ahead. He couldn't believe his blessings: finding her at church, falling in love, the happy year of courtship, the pleasure of rescuing her from her neglectful family; and

Pauline Theda Davison

Robert Davison

today marrying the love of his life. God had answered his prayers.

It had been challenging to learn his trade and start his own business. In March he'd be 27. Davison's, Inc. was running smoothly, supporting his family members, and after today, his beautiful young wife. She had brought such sparkle into his life, even calling him Bob, instead of the old-fashioned Robert his family used. Their new house would soon be completed. Life was amazing.

Pauline looked at her astonishing self in the mirror. The satin wedding gown draped perfectly down her slim figure to her satin clad toes, and her cloud-like veil gently followed as she turned in a happy pirouette. Shiny, dark hair in an elegant updo and sapphire-blue eyes twinkled back at her merry laugh. How had this happened, this wondrous miracle of love? Her prayers had been fulfilled with a handsome, funny, intelligent and loving man, seven years her senior, and as serious about his Christian beliefs as she was about hers. The year she had asked for when he proposed had been twelve months of delight, as they grew together. Now, at 20, she had no doubt that their marriage was divinely blessed, and she could hardly wait to become Robert Edward Davison's bride that afternoon.

She was a "blushing bride" for sure, after the embarrassing talk about female hygiene with her stepmother that morning. Her wedding gift from Katharine Theda had been a douching kit and explicit instructions about how to use it. Awkward, but considering the source, not unusual.

It was not long now. She twirled again. She was going to wed her best friend, the man God had prepared for her, her

Pauline Virginia Theda

Prince Charming! Life was incredible! Pauline walked down the aisle on the arm of her father, peeking through her veil at Robert, waiting at the altar. The organ music swelled, and the scent of white gardenias in her bouquet made her dizzy with the joy of the moment. Paul Theda lay his daughter's hand in Robert's palm, and stepped aside, symbolic of her old existence retreating before the new. Robert held her hand firmly, promising to treasure her for the rest of their lives. The vows were made, and the rings exchanged.

On January 20, 1939, Pauline Theda became Mrs. Robert Edward Davison.

That night, as they dressed for bed, Pauline was trembling and anxious. Her stepmother had prepared her for the ablution after, not the marriage bed before. Pauline wasn't ready for the mystery of marital union. Robert was kind and understanding. He was excited to end his virginity, but instead held her with tenderness and love. Though Pauline slept with relief that night, Robert spent the hours awake, tightly gripping the edges of the mattress.

For the honeymoon, he took his bride for a month-long road trip. They started with Death Valley and relatives in California. Then, their Ford coupe carried them through the Southwest, from Las Vegas to New Orleans, for a quick visit to Pauline's brother, Kenneth. On their trip home, they traveled to other states and routes they had skipped. After a month, they happily returned to the house he'd built for her in North Beach, next to Pop and Nana's.

As a young couple, they enjoyed the fun of being newlyweds and the playfulness of their group of friends. The group even bought property on Snoqualmie Pass, as a joint investment. In future years Dad would buy it from the others and build a cabin.

But Robert was yet to find out the scope of Pauline's story.

CHAPTER NINE
Grandma Alice, Invisible
1918—1936

Dad married a sweetheart who came from a place of mystery. Not even she knew her true background. Except for a few hints, there was little to pass on to us about her ancestry. The backdrop of callousness she had lived was kept from us children. All we knew was her heart to give us a perfect childhood and her spirit of care for her family and anyone needing help. I would never have guessed her backstory.

Once I found Mom's history, it became clear why she covered Dad's decline for so long. She deeply understood what loving protection would mean to a vulnerable soul.

I never knew my grandmother, Alice Theda. She was hidden away long before I was born. After giving birth to my mom in 1918, Grandma Alice doted on her baby for three years and then disappeared from Mom's life. Over the following decades when my mom reached out for more information, she was always rebuffed with silence. When I was older she and I continued her search. Rare photos and records gave only a glimmer of Grandma Alice, so I kept digging.

My maternal line, forced to swim upstream, developed very strong women: on my maternal side my mom, Pauline; Grandma Alice; great-grandmother, Elizabeth; and my great-great-grandmother, MaryAnn Spain.

Grandma Alice's grandparents, William and MaryAnn Spain, were immigrants from Ireland, who arrived in Wisconsin just before the Civil War. William Spain served as a lieutenant, fighting for the North. After the war, he returned to Portage, Columbia County, Wisconsin, and set up a law practice. One afternoon in 1869, he was confronted by Barney Britt, a disgruntled neighboring farmer and fellow veteran from William Spain's military unit. Jealous of the Captain's rise in rank, Britt "accosted him in the street over a long-standing dispute," the newspaper of the day reported.

"You dirty, damned son-of-a-bitch," shouted the angry former private, the index finger of his right hand pointed at Spain like a gun. *"I've had enough of your*

William Henry Spain

hornswoggle. And now you've taken to defending a murderous outlaw, Pat Wildrick! You think you're high and mighty, better'n us townsfolk, but you're nothing but a boot-licking reprobate."

"Pig-headed scoundrel," shouted Captain Spain, my great-great-grandfather. "You're a pustulant canker on the ass of the Union, and I'm fed up with your cursed slander. I've a mind to teach you a lesson!"

Irish tempered great-great-grandfather marched down the road to his house and took down his gun box. He picked up the .44 caliber Colt revolver left from the war, made sure it was loaded, and strode out the door. The farmer had followed him and stood across the road hurling new insults. Great-Great-Grandfather raised the revolver and shot the father of eight dead.

An angry crowd began to form, shouting, "Hang him!" The townspeople were already furious with William Spain for serving as defense attorney for Pat Wildrick, the meanest outlaw in the Territory. Wildrick sat in jail awaiting trial for killing prominent businessman, Schuyler Gates, father of six, and the only eyewitness to Wildrick's latest crime.

Seeking protection from the irate citizens, William Spain tried to turn himself in and was locked up in the jail. The mob grew larger, knocked down the door, dragged my great-great-grandfather to a tree in the middle of town, threw a rope around his neck, and lynched him. The next day, the mob broke into the jail again, tied up the sheriff and his deputy, and hung Wildrick from a tree in a nearby ravine.

Finding a Hollywood movie script in my history was a

surprise. One hundred fifty years later I'd seen and read this plot often, but the anguish and suffering of my own family was personal. Wives and children of the three dead men were suddenly abandoned. It took brave and strong women to struggle on.

My great-great-grandmother, Mary Ann Spain, was such a woman and trudged alone to raise her daughter Elizabeth, and three siblings. When Elizabeth was old enough to marry, she chose John Galligan of Ireland. He ran off after the birth of their fourth daughter, Alice, so I know nothing of him. Elizabeth supported the family by teaching piano lessons. Because John deserted the family, Elizabeth did not baptize Alice in the Catholic religion as she had Alice's sisters Florence, Anna, and Margaret. My mom inherited Alice's Protestantism, though the rest of the Galligans were Catholic.

Baby Pauline's black curls wriggled as she fretted in her crib; perspiration glistened on her small, sleeping body. The hot desert breeze coming through the open tent flap did little to reduce the heat inside, so her mother had dressed her in only a diaper. Outside, the sun slipped behind the chaparral-covered hills, but it would be a while before the burning earth began to cool. Alice fanned her little girl until the air was cooler outside than inside, then took her to the cooking tent to start dinner.

My mom was born on November 26, 1918, fifteen days after the signing of the treaty that ended World War I. While the world celebrated the armistice in Europe, in Minneapolis, Minnesota, Paul and Alice Theda celebrated the birth of their baby girl, Pauline Virginia. Named after her father, Pauline had her Mom's Irish charm, with curly

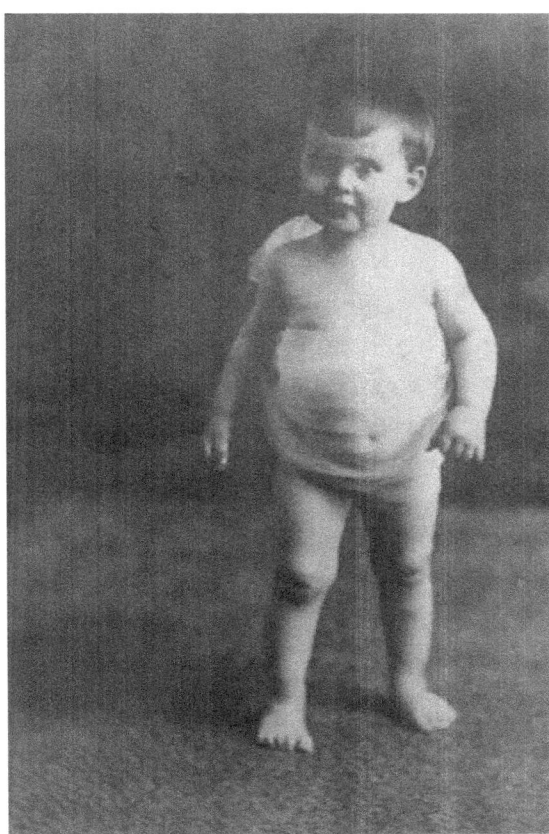

Pauline Virginia Theda

black hair, deep blue eyes, and a happy nature. A happy nature that survived a childhood resembling the 1905 novel, *The Little Princess*—times of happy highs and lonely lows. Pauline grew up with a love of travel that lasted a lifetime, and when she died at 92, she had visited every continent on earth. That love of travel began before her first birthday when her parents moved from Minnesota to Fort Worth, Texas. Twelve months later, in 1920, her father and his three brothers, John, Will, and Albert, decided to pool their money and move from Texas to California's booming San Fernando Valley. They bought land in an area of small, irrigated farm plots near the town of Burbank—land which later became home to the movie studios. Alice again packed up her household and baby Pauline and moved to California where the families planned to live in tents while working to improve their farmland.

How do you set up your household in tents? Here's what I imagine. In one, Alice set up their sleeping quarters with beds, chests, vanities, and chifforobes, like an earthy boudoir. In another, she set up storage and provisions for cooking, an icebox, kitchen preparation area, and a table and chairs for their daily suppers. A third tent held farm supplies and equipment. Water came from a pump in the yard, and a 'biffy,' was perched behind the tents.

Alice spent most days watching two-year-old Pauline, doing household chores, and tending the large, fast-growing garden. She spent much of her time over a fire. Cooking was done outdoors in big pots which hung from a wooden frame over a smoky blaze, or using a reflector oven or frying pan, grilling only when she had fresh meat.

She cooked breakfasts in the blushing early morning, dinners in mean midday heat or rain, and suppers in cooling or cold evenings. Once a week, she would fill a big tub with fire-heated water and wash clothes on a

Alice Alberta Galligan Theda

washboard. The next day she'd iron the sun-dried clothes with a fire-heated flatiron.

Other days were for sewing and mending clothes, weeding and caring for the lush vegetable beds, or occasional trips to town. Twice a month, she filled the big tub with water for baths, the three of them using the same water, beginning with Pauline.

The California sun grew giant tomatoes, carrots, spinach, green beans, potatoes, corn, melons, and berries from the fertile soil of the big garden plot, and apples, pears, apricots, and peaches from the fruit trees already on the land. All this and more, Alice would preserve for the winter months. In the cool of early morning, she would set the copper kettle over the fire to heat and sterilize the canning jars in the boiling water. Next, she'd wash and prepare the contents, fill and seal the jars, and place them in the kettle to boil. She had 25 minutes to get the next batch ready. She also made jams and jellies in the big black pots over the fire, then finished the jars in a hot water bath. Apples, apricots, pears, and peaches, she dried in the sun.

In the summer, temperatures could run as high as 114° in the valley, though stayed mainly in the 80s and 90s. From November through March, the rain would fall intermittently, one storm could bring as much as seven inches and flash floods, with an average temperature of about 55°, but known to go as low as the 20s.

Like the smoke and dust, the flying insects were another misery. Flies, no-see-ums and mosquitoes were always buzzing around the food, eyes, ears, bare skin, and baby Pauline. Alice placed the baby under netting to sleep, but as Pauline grew old enough to play all day, she became an insect smorgasbord like everyone else.

More fearful were the varmints—snakes, scorpions, spiders—and the scavengers, like mice and rats, nutria and coyotes. Trying to keep a baby safe and healthy in a tent, in the San Fernando Valley's 1920s, would have been a relentless struggle

After a year of rough living, Grandpa Paul placed Grandma Alice in a California mental institution, no explanation given. Was it her difficult lifestyle, a nervous breakdown, a combination, or what? Then he took three-year-old Pauline by train from California to his brother's home in Wenatchee, Washington. It was the fall of 1921. Grandma Alice was 28. Mom had no idea that for the next six years she would live with five-year-old Cousin Delores, Uncle Will, and Aunt Olive Theda.

Little Pauline loved that trip with her daddy, which launched her life-long love of trains. In her 90s, when she no longer liked to drive long distances, she would visit me by rail. On one trip, she was eating lunch in the dining car, and forgot to get off at her stop. As I hurried to pick her up at the next station, I was worried she would be frightened and anxious. When I found her, she was sitting alone in the empty station, delighted that she had gotten to take the extra ride.

Mysteriously, soon after her commitment, Grandma Alice was discharged from the mental hospital back into the care of her husband, Paul. After a short time, she was recommitted, pregnant with Pauline's brother Kenneth. He was born in the asylum in 1922 and lived there for his first year. He was probably not the only baby there bringing normalcy to his mother and the staff. How surreal it must have been to hear baby laughter as well as patients' wails ringing through the sorrowful halls. Some asylums of that day were dreadful, but Alice was in the Metropolitan State Hospital in Norwalk, *Southern California's only mental hospital, with a good and progressive reputation in the 1920s. When he was weaned, Kenneth went to live with Alice's sister, Margaret Nagel, and her family in Portland, Oregon, where he was raised for four years with his cousin, Jack.

Sometime later, Paul left Alice in the California institution and returned to the Pacific Northwest, to live as a single man in a Seattle boarding house. He was intrigued by the landlady's daughter, Katharine. After a short courtship he proposed to her and filed for divorce from Alice. Grandfather Paul married Katharine the day after the divorce was final.

Imagine the despair of being abandoned and far from your family, in a mental asylum, with the ever-present clanking of locked doors and cries of other patients. Imagine your beautiful, huggable, sweet-smelling babies taken from you forever. Imagine the humiliation, overwhelming emptiness, and excruciating pain of being discarded by someone you loved and trusted. It would be hell on earth, more than most could bear. Three days after Paul's remarriage, Alice died in the institution at the age of 33. Her sister Margaret took her to Portland, Oregon where she was buried in the Catholic Cemetery. Alice's divorce settlement and inheritance went to her children and were used to pay family expenses through the Depression.

Robbed of her history, Mom searched for information over the years, but the closet door was locked so tightly that

Mom didn't even know her grandmother's maiden name was Spain. She thought our ancestors came from there. She also didn't know that her grandmother Elizabeth was alive in Wisconsin until 1949, when I was seven. Even in her forties, Grandpa Theda refused to share any information with his daughter.

Elderly Aunt Fanny, Uncle Albert's wife, told Mom that Alice was a nymphomaniac. The definition in those days ran anywhere from flirting or wearing perfume to attract men, to physical deviance. Hard to know if Fanny had dementia, or if that was part of Alice's diagnosis.

Grandma Alice was treated like an old coat, worn out and discarded for a new one. Her death certificate states that she suffered from dementia praecox (schizophrenia). It wasn't until 1973 that opioid receptors were discovered, and it took until 1987 for Prozac to be developed. In the 1920s, Alice's disgraced family tried to erase her. Very few photos remain to prove she existed.

Brain research has advanced since 1921, helping many locked in private torment. Public empathy and compassion are far behind. One moment those with mental illness have the attention because of some violent act, and the next, they are ignored or shunned like biblical lepers. This stigma continues today. Grandma Alice, you were just a tiny drop in a relentless river of despair.

*Grandma Alice's place of confinement was the Metropolitan State Hospital in Southern California. Her Death Certificate number is 3268 California Death Index.

CHAPTER TEN
Little Pauline
1927—1939

The joy that Robert saw in Pauline when he met her came from her sunny childhood in Wenatchee, six years that fostered her sweet nature. Mom scattered petals of happiness wherever she went, gleefully paraphrasing Ecclesiastes. "I cast my bread upon the water, and it comes back buttered." It was a surprise for us girls to find that this bouquet of happiness bloomed from being fertilized in bullshit.

"Look out!" shouted nine-year-old Pauline. "Outlaws are hiding behind the barn!" She galloped her make-believe palomino toward the apple orchard, while her Cousin Delores, two years older, turned her imaginary stallion around and followed. The two had been playing horses in the backyard all morning, oblivious of the beautiful, blue, sun-spangled Columbia River in the distance. Later, they might go for a swim when the afternoon became too hot.

Grand hills, like sleeping giants, circle the Wenatchee Valley's leafy orchard country. Nestled into sedimentary

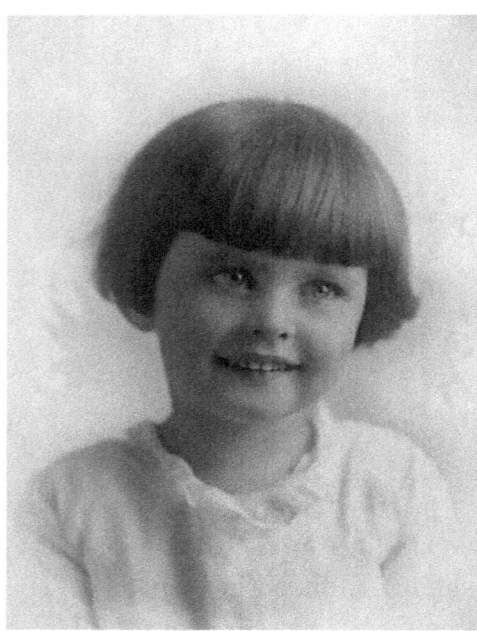
Pauline Virginia Theda, 3

rock, carved by ancient icebergs, this irrigated oasis sits at the base of Washington's Cascade Mountains.

An agricultural basin split down the middle by a silvery ribbon of winding river, flourishes with fruit in hot summers and ticking sprinklers. In winter, the valley huddles under soft blankets of snow, eager to burst forth into spring shoots and blossoms.

Separated from her mother and father and delivered to strange relatives in this far-away place, three-year-old Pauline reacted as she would for the rest of her life come thick or thin. She thrived. She was blessed with a nature that could find the gold among the dross, and she tucked this gift and her years in Wenatchee close to her heart when luck changed.

Her welcome was heartwarming. Uncle Will, Aunt Olive, and Cousin Dolores embraced her as a dear member of their family. You know how it feels to be loved: how when you look up, someone's eyes are smiling at you; how when you're having trouble, like tying your shoes, someone's there to help; or, when you ask a silly question, someone always answers. That's how Little Pauline felt with her new family. Her father visited a few times, but her roots attached to her new soil.

She grew up in a healthy environment and delighted in the outdoor surroundings of the Wenatchee Valley: wild, dry countryside tamed by the flowing Columbia River, sun tanning summers of swimming, floating the river, swinging under shady trees. Freezing winters begged for sledding, skiing, forts, and snowball fights. Uncle Will worked as manager of Fisher Flour Mill, grinding grain from hundreds of acres of wheat grown east of Wenatchee, and her Uncle John and wife Florence also lived nearby running their restaurant, Theda's Pantry. Mom's six years in Wenatchee were, "the happiest of my childhood," she said.

"Girls, it's time to come in," Aunt Olive called from the house. "Your father's here, Pauline. Wash your hands and faces and come say hello." Her father had come to take her home. It was 1927.

Pauline was too little to remember much about her first trip over the mountains, except the excitement of seeing snow. This time, when she was nine, the snow piled at the summit of Snoqualmie Pass had melted into dirty patches beside the tracks, and the excitement of snow was replaced by the excitement of meeting her five-year-old brother, Kenneth. She'd seen him only in photographs, as she was living in Wenatchee when he was born. She would also meet her father's new wife, Katharine. He'd built a house for the family on Magnolia Hill, near downtown Seattle, and this is where they all would live. The house had bedrooms for everyone, a sunny kitchen for Etta, their housekeeper, and a one-car garage in the basement.

Stepmother, Katharine Crane Theda, was blonde, well dressed, and a professional woman. No one would guess her background from her formal demeanor. As a six-month-old baby, she had been put up for adoption in 1893, when her mother, Blanche Farrington, followed the baby's father, George Stevenson, to the Alaskan goldfields. Baby Katharine was adopted and raised by the Crane family. Not fond of her adoptive parents, as an adult she looked for her birth mother and found her running a Seattle boarding house. There, Katharine met Paul Theda. When they married and moved into their new Seattle home, Katharine brought along her newly found mother, Blanche, to help with the children.

As a stepmother, Katharine Theda lived up to the stereotype, with no empathy for her newly acquired stepchildren. Grandpa Theda thought he was giving Pauline and Kenny a new mother to replace Alice, but instead of motherly love came cross intolerance. Regarded as weeds rather than sweet blossoms, they were unaware of being closely watched for signs of Alice's illness.

Katharine was domineering and the rules in the Theda household were strict. Both parents worked, he as an accountant, and she as a typist. After school, Pauline and Kenny were not allowed to come into the house until their parents got home several hours later, even though Etta and Grandma Farrington were there. The sister and little brother played in the grassy backyard, with bushes for their restroom. When it rained, they played in the cement-floored basement garage, domain of the family's small, yappy dog. Mom's aversion to dogs came from there. On Pauline's errands to the basement, the small, nervous dog would bark at the intrusion, and she would be punished for teasing it. Typically, her innocent actions were viewed as mischief.

One day Pauline watched as a little boy came walking down the street to her house. She recognized him as a third-grade classmate.

"Hi, Pauline," he said with a smile, "I came to see if you could play after school."

As soon as he reached her, she anxiously pulled him behind the retaining wall in the garage driveway, so he couldn't be seen from the house above. "I'm not allowed to have friends over," she apologized. "Please go home, or I'll get in trouble. If anybody sees you I'll be punished."

He looked disappointed, turned, and headed back up the sidewalk. "See you at school tomorrow," he waved. Pauline quickly ducked into the backyard.

Later, at dinner, Katharine asked coldly, "Who was the little boy Grandma Farrington saw you playing with after school today, Pauline? You know I've asked you not to invite anyone after school."

"I told him to go home," Pauline looked down at her hands in her lap. "I didn't ask him. I'm sorry he came."

"What do you think, Paul?" Katharine asked her new husband.

"I think you need to obey your mother, Pauline." Her father's eyes looked disappointed. "There will be no dessert for you tonight."

In Katharine's eyes, Pauline was a rule-breaker, a nuisance, a disagreeable itch. My mom was not allowed to participate in school groups, extracurricular activities, or Girl Scouts. "When invited," her parents told her, "say no."

She was taught formal behavior and expected to use it. She knew the proper placement of tableware and glassware, their use, and to keep her left hand in her lap while eating. The material and social behaviors of life were imperative to her stepmother, the matters of children, trivial. Her value lay in the inheritance from her mother which paid for Pauline and Kenny's room and board through the Depression years.

In July of 1927, beloved baby sister, Kathy, or Bonnie as Katharine called her, was born. Kathy was pampered and preferred, though she dearly loved her big sister, Pauline. Although nine years younger, Kathy's devotion never flagged, and when she grew old enough to realize her preferential treatment, she was embarrassed by the unfairness of it for the rest of her life. She and Mom loved and supported each other until Mom died in 2011.

In 1962, Kathy published the novel *All the Tea in China*, created from a family secret she overheard. She loosely based the life of the main character on the callous treatment Mom received as an adolescent. It is a great book and enlightening. It helped me understand the pressure my mom endured.

Mom has always loved working in the kitchen whipping up treats. It was a large part of who she was and added pounds to our waistlines. During her Magnolia years, the kitchen was a safe and friendly place. She found cheer among the baking smells, steamy pots, and the warmth of Etta, the family housekeeper, who taught Pauline how to cook. It was a refuge Mom cherished, and Etta's recipe cards were family treasures.

My family spent summer vacations together in our

trailer. We'd visit Lake Chelan, the ocean, Lake Wenatchee, Montana, or Disneyland. Disneyland opened in 1955 among the berry fields and orange groves of Anaheim, California, and for our summer vacation in 1956, we stayed in a trailer park across a strawberry field from the parking lot.

In contrast, when the Theda family went on summer vacation, they would drop young Pauline and Kenny off with a married couple who ran a motel in Kingston, a ferry boat ride from Seattle. Then Paul and Katharine would go on their trip with little Kathy. Mom said the couple was nice and it was wonderful being on the salty beach of Puget Sound. I imagine the freedom from harshness must have been liberating. At the end of the Theda family vacation, they would retrieve their extra children.

Pauline and Kenny had better luck as adolescents when they were sent to visit family in Oregon each summer. Aunt Margaret, Grandma Alice's sister, and Uncle Frank Nagel rented a cottage at Jantzen Beach and doted on their niece and nephew. Aunt Margaret even hired a playmate for Pauline during the vacations, while Kenny and cousin Jack played together. Happy photos remain of those seaside summers.

Pauline was not permitted social activities, but she and her brother were allowed to attend church where they found lifelong strength. Their parents never joined them.

In 1936, she graduated from high school in the top of her class, then went to work for a company selling window shade supplies, where she would meet Dad.

While she worked for the shade supplier, she lived at home. Best friend, Maryann, asked Pauline to be a bridesmaid at her wedding and Pauline was delighted because her parents, Paul and Katharine, were invited, too. It was an exciting time with parties and wedding showers, dress fittings, and luncheons. The day of the wedding, Pauline donned her bridesmaid dress, pinched her cheeks for color, and descended the stairs to the living room where her parents were reading. Putting on her coat she said, "I have to go early but I'll meet you there."

"We're not going," Katharine said behind her newspaper.

Pauline thought she must have misunderstood. "What?" she said.

"We're not going. We didn't get an invitation," the hard voice still hidden behind the raised newspaper.

Kathy remembers the time because their behavior cut Mom so deeply she cried for two days. Embarrassment. Despair. Shame. She would never be good enough for her parents.

Time passed and the boy she'd been dating, Gene, proposed. She declined. I'm amazed she didn't marry just to get out of the house. Instead, she waited for the fairytale ending.

Just after Kenny graduated from high school, he broke his hip while wrestling with a friend. His body cast had a bar between his legs to keep them apart, which also served to flip him from front to back. Pauline spent the summer at his bedside until the cast was removed. One leg proved shorter than the other. The resulting limp dashed his plans to join the military, so he joined the reserves instead, and served his wartime in Alaska.

Kathy told me that Katharine did not like boys and

treated Kenny worse than Pauline. Stuck in Kathy's mind is a scene as an eight-year-old, standing with her parents at the bottom of the stairs that led to the bedrooms, looking up as Kenny, with a dislocated hip, painfully crawled to get to the top. She kept thinking, "Why doesn't somebody help him?" Finally, when he was almost there, Katharine gave permission for Paul to go help him.

Pauline and Kenneth never lived near each other as adults, he in the South and she in the North, but they felt a close bond throughout their lives. He grew into a fine man and Southern Baptist minister, and remembered his relationship with his parents as ordinary, different from Mom's recollections. This was toward the end of his life when his dementia may have affected his recall. He failed to realize that activities with his father, like joining the Scouts and attending their functions, did not exist for Pauline.

After her less than fulfilling youth, Mom's resilience was remarkable. Mentally stuffing her teenage years, she kept her nine-year-old's exuberance that animated our lives until she left us just shy of her ninety-third birthday. Treating her parents with grace until they died proved her power of forgiveness. Dad found her soft-hearted approach, sunny spirit, and loving nature irresistible, but he was tormented in later years as he slowly learned the sweep of her neglect and stood guard at the gate of Mom's past to keep embarrassing ghosts from slipping out.

When my sisters and I learned more, we thought of Grandma Theda as Cruella de Vil, shallow, domineering, and manipulative, and Grandpa Theda, as Caspar Milquetoast, weak and submissive. Cruella and Casper are exaggerations; my grandparents lived the best their flaws allowed. Grandpa Theda could be warm and funny, and Grandma Theda could be thoughtful with small gifts. But the basic fact remains that Mom and our family mattered little in their lives.

As children, the few formal dinners we had with Grandma and Grandpa Theda were as pleasurable as standing in a corner with your nose to the wall. The only memory I have of those visits is a feeling of unease in their house, and my grandfather's jolly laugh as he sat at the dinner table sharpening the knife to cut the roast. Alice and I were primped, paraded, and expected to be "seen and not heard," like our mother. Alice was three when she got into Grandma Theda's powder and spread it around their bathroom, the only pleasant memory that exists. Dad probably secretly enjoyed it, but Mom must have suffered extreme embarrassment. I don't think she ever surrendered to the fact that even with a good husband and a beautiful family, she'd never measure up. Kenny and Kathy moved far away. Mom, like an abandoned child, stayed close, and always tried to please her mother and father.

I've never understood why Grandpa Theda didn't stick up for his daughter. He had a playful nature, and my mom felt his love. The term "pussy-whipped" comes to mind. Katharine was his "Kat o' nine tails."

CHAPTER ELEVEN
Young Dad
1942—1958

I awoke to a noise by my window. Opening my baby eyes, I heard a low voice. "Psst...come over here." Crawling curiously to the end of the crib, I was lifted by strong arms, out the window, and into the misty, grey afternoon. Held tightly as we crossed the driveway, I could smell the cooking cabbage before we entered the kitchen, where my grandmother and my auntie were in the middle of fixing dinner.

"Hello, my dearie girl," Auntie Letha smiled at me. "Did you have a

"Pop" Phillip Sheridan Davison, 100

nice nap?"

Nana said nothing as she peeled the potatoes. Pop put me down in my high-chair. "I told her mom I'd bring her back before dinner."

When I look in the mirror, I see my grandfather's eyes looking back at me, light blue, with deep pools of playfulness, and an eagerness to best life. I met him during his seventh decade—where I am now—and grew up with his brightness coloring my universe. Captive of his blithe spirit from the beginning, he lived across the driveway and would spirit me out of my bedroom window, and into his house, like a magic trick. Over the years, he became both grandfather and surrogate father.

Exactly ten months after Pearl Harbor, I was born October 7, 1942. Named after my Mom, Pauline Virginia Davison, I was called Polly to avoid confusion. When I was older I changed the spelling to Pauli, more true to my given name. Dad was the baby of six children, so I was celebrated by a multiplicity of grandparents, aunts, uncles, and cousins who cuddled, coddled,

"Polly" Pauline Virginia Davison

and overindulged me. I'm told I was a bright and busy baby. Before I was three Mom found me sitting on top of the freestanding ironing board. It remains a mystery how I got there. I have sparse memories of that period, a tapestry of feelings and family stories, opaque through the mists of time. There is the very early and shadowy memory of sitting on a pile of blankets, in the dark, in the bed of a pickup truck that was covered by a hand-made, windowless, wooden canopy. The air is cool; small beams of light stream from a space between the canopy doors, open a crack, to prevent us from being poisoned by carbon monoxide. My daddy and Nana are in the cab. Sitting in the darkness with Mama and me are my Auntie Queenie, her grandson Joey, Pop, and Auntie Letha. We are on our way to visit Uncle Paul in California. Part memory, part lore, it tells me that my family loved to travel enough to do it in the roughest and most dangerous conditions.

"It's Daddy. I see him!" I squealed, squinting my two-year-old eyes against the radiant light, his features backlit and dark.

Daddy came strolling down the long, bright skybridge of the Seattle Ferry Terminal, and I ran to meet him. It's a hazy memory, and I was very small, but I remember the joy in my heart.

My daddy was jolly and fun. He carried me on his shoulders, and I rode his horsey back. I called him Uncle Robert for a while because that's what my older cousins called him. When the United States was thrown into World War II, he went to work painting ships at the Puget Sound Naval Shipyard. At 32, he was exempt from military service, but Dad wanted to protect his nephew Wally,

Queenie's unruly older son. Two years earlier, Wally, at 17, had married his 15-year-old girlfriend, Jean. She was pregnant when Wally received his draft notice. Patriotic, yet wanting to keep his nephew safe from harm, Dad stepped in, designated Wally as the irreplaceable head of Dad's business, and took Wally's place in the war effort. With Dad's mentorship, Wally assumed the management of Davison's, helped by his mom, Queenie. Then, Dad began the daily ferry ride to the Bremerton Navy Yard to paint ships.

The commute between Seattle and Bremerton was two hours each day. Grapeview, the family getaway on the Olympic Peninsula, was much closer to the shipyard, so Mom, Dad, and I moved there in 1944 to save the round trip.

Mom set up housekeeping in the cabin, and I ran free through the long grasses, picking grapes and playing on the

Dad, bathing in Grapeview before work at the Puget Sound Ship Yard

beach. Toward the end of the war, Wally was finally taken into the Army and helped liberate the concentration camps, Dad told me. We returned home from Grapeview for Alice's birth in July. Two months later, on September 2, 1945, the formal Japanese delegation signed the instrument of surrender, which ended WWII. Dad put away his paintbrush and returned to the Shop. The Battleship Missouri, on which the surrender was signed, ended up as a museum at the Bremerton Naval Ship Yard.

Almost three years of my own spotlight, and along came Alice. She held the center of attention, and I was unhappy and felt betrayed. I pinched a friend's baby as a substitute for mine, then hid when the baby cried. It felt good. Pop seemed my only champion. He understood. Especially when we moved.

Dad was 36, happy, and full of fun and laughter. He loved his family, hot dogs, cocoa, picnics, and storytelling. While I rode his bouncing foot, he'd tell Alice and me stories about Little Red Deer, the Indian brave, or Chief Falling Rock—the name borrowed from the road signs on Snoqualmie Pass. He amused himself with jokes he made from the unique names of our state's cities—Seattle, Spokane, Tacoma, Issaquah, and Stillaguamish.

"There were three Indian maidens living at home," he'd begin. "A young Indian brave knocked on their door. 'I've come to Sea-Attle,' he said.

"Attle isn't home," Spoke-Ann. "Would you like to Take-Oma?" Smiling with humor he'd go on, "When Is-a-quah, not a quah?" Dad's green eyes sparkling with amusement, "when it's Still-a-guamish." A boyish chuckle slipped out.

Dad's creativity was innate. It rolled from him like

breath, easy and natural, as irrepressible as waves seeking the shore. It flowed through the years, as overlooked as his beautiful Irish-tenor voice, unnoticed until as adults, we heard him singing in church. However, melody still filled the background of our childhood. Both Dad and Mom whistled their happiness like beautiful birdsong. Their music soared with dips and swirls, swoops and trills, and the pulsing strands were lilting, not too fast, and not too slow, more ethereal than a high and lovely flute. Mom whistled throughout the day, and Dad when he was home nights and weekends. Sometimes, together, they twined their notes in melodious duets. Classics like "Brahms Lullaby," tunes of the time like "Deep Purple," or folk melodies like "My Wild Irish Rose," filled our days—a philharmonic treasure taken for granted until we grew up.

 Dad's whistling spilled over into home movie nights. When he bought a camera and 8mm projector to shoot family movies, the package included two black-and-white cartoons, "Puss In Boots" and "Pepe Le Pew." Alice and I laughed with delight when he whistled sound effects and made-up dialogue as the cartoons played. "Do it again! Do it again," we two little girls would clap and shout at the end of each cartoon, and, obligingly, he would.

 He was a dedicated photographer and shot years of family slides and films, filling movie nights with hilarity and nostalgia. I'd grin as my sisters shrieked at the movie of me, a small happy three-year-old, holding a wriggling garter snake by the tail. Dad captured five decades of family memories, as well as every trip he took. Digitizing a thousand of his slides took a couple of years; I've yet to start on his films, but the time he devoted to family history deserves to be honored.

Spontaneity spiked Dad's fun, whether a picnic, a song, or a surprise. In 1946, he brought home a new Ford, "Woodie" station wagon. It had beautiful, varnished-mahogany inserts with trim on the outside and an interior of honey-colored, bird's-eye maple. Inside, golden slats, set about two inches apart, covered the ceiling from front to back. Running perpendicular, or side to side, matching struts crossed the slats, and were fastened to the sides at eighteen-inch intervals. The pattern left small, two-inch tunnels under each strut, giving Dad an idea.

He sanded a 2x6 inch board, small enough for my four-year-old tush and cut a hole in each end. Then he ran a long cord down through one hole, under the seat and up through the other hole and tied each end to a strut on the ceiling. Unencumbered by seat belt rules, I had a swing in the aisle to the back seat, where on our next trip, I happily swung my way to California. It was a big step up from the previous wood box-covered bed of an old pick-up that I traveled in when I was tiny.

On both trips, we picnicked our way to California. With little money for restaurants, Dad was happy to buy a loaf of bread, some bologna, and mustard, and maybe a quart of milk to go with Mom's home-made cookies. Fruit picked up at fruit stands completed our meals. Dad loved the spontaneity, simplicity, and thrift of eating al fresco, whether on long trips or short. Whether visiting Mount Rainier meadows or the slapping shores of Puget Sound, or most of the Washington state parks, we always took a picnic. Our family sat on the grassy mound at the Puyallup Fair entrance each year, eating our sandwiches and cookies, while I enviously watched other fairgoers eat hot dogs, burgers, and cotton candy.

The Davison family's favorite gathering spot in Seattle was the Woodland Park Zoo, near where they first lived. Under tall fir trees sheltering wooden picnic tables, Dad's relatives met for celebrations, birthdays, and holidays. In the early days, the Zoo was free, and I would go in and howl to the monkeys who howled back, causing a wonderful commotion. We girls and our cousins chased each other over well-kept fields or played hide-and-seek among the trees, while the grownups shared the big potluck meal.

When baby sister Carol arrived on December 22, 1949, Dad now had three children and a growing business. More responsibility meant more work, so he started spending extra evenings away from home making calls on prospective customers. Sometimes he would take Alice or me with him. Happily sitting in the car, parked on a quiet, tree-lined Ballard street, I'd work on my dot-to-dot book while he measured for new linoleum or showed samples of carpet. With the car's window rolled down, the smell of fresh-mown grass or a waft of supper casserole would come floating on the soft breeze of dusk turning to evening. I sat in the summer twilight, the silence broken only by an occasional bird call. I was nine or ten and proud to be with Dad and the center of his attention. I didn't know that these outings were to get Alice or me out of the house each time Mom lost a full-term baby after Carol was born.

Sometimes on these trips together, he'd let me sit on his lap and drive. I was a curious scalawag, a quality I probably inherited from Pop, and wondered what it would feel like to steer right or left instead of just straight ahead. I yanked the wheel to the left one day and scared the bejeebers out of Dad. He grabbed the wheel. "Don't ever do that again!" His voice alarmed. "Do you realize you could have caused an accident? It was just lucky that no other cars were coming." I was properly apologetic but secretly delighted at my daring.

To extend his picnics overnight, Dad saved enough money to buy a travel trailer to tow behind our Woodie station wagon. In 1950, our wanderings began; the picnics rolled on, trailer attached.

Beautiful, blue Lake Crescent, in Washington's Olympic National Forest, provided a successful trial run, so the following summer, Dad set out to seek the treasured Montana homestead of his memory. Carol was six months old when christened with wanderdust. At each campground, she sat happily in a cardboard box, teething on a piece of celery, watching Mom fix dinner for the five of

Polly, Robert, Carol, and Alice Davison, 1950

us. With trips to Montana in 1950, and again in 1952, Dad taught us family lore early, and first-hand.

Montana's wildlife was abundant; Alice and I saw buffalo, moose, antelope, and bear up close. One evening, traveling at dusk, I jolted in my seat when our station wagon accidentally bumped a brown bear from behind as he was running down the road. We gave him a big boost and watched him scurry off into the woods, shocked but unharmed.

"Mama! Alice is on my side," I sang from the back seat of the station wagon. "Am not," replied five-year-old Alice.

"You two quit fighting," Mama said. "Look out the window and watch for buffalo." As the travel trailer rolled through Glacier National Park, the scenery, fascinating to adults, had become monotonous to five and seven-year-olds.

Carol Louise Davison

"I have to go to the bathroom," Alice said, wanting a distraction.

Daddy pulled onto a large, graveled area, and parked next to the woods. Alice clambered from the back seat and squatted where Mama had made a private space, next to her open door, facing the trees. Alice went about her business when a movement on the left caught my eye and a scruffy brown bear lumbered out of the woods, nose sniffing the air. It started up the short incline toward our idling car. "A BEAR!" I screamed, bouncing on my seat. "It's coming! It's coming!" Daddy looked up from his map, Mama looked up from Alice. The terror in my voice drove Alice to finish in fright, and leap onto Mama's lap, just as the curious bear reached the other side of the slamming door. Mama frantically rolled up her window to keep the bear's nose from poking in. Dad shifted the Woodie into gear, and off we went, shouting with gladness and adrenalin.

Dad loved Montana and returned several times, but he spent much of his time exploring the Southwest. He had no interest in Europe; he said there were enough things to see in the United States. Disneyland became a favorite destination where he'd take in the excitement through the fresh eyes of his children, then grandchildren. His child's heart reveled in sharing it over and over. Once he was on a trailer trip, he'd make it last for several weeks, knowing his sisters, Letha and Queenie, would capably manage the Shop. Dad hated to come home.

CHAPTER TWELVE
Edmonds
1946—1958

Family growing, and chasing his dream, Dad bought a five-acre farm, ten miles up the coast, and moved us to the town of Edmonds. An eye-popping view of the Kingston ferry and the Olympic Mountains, a cherry and apple orchard, pastures, and a big barn, fit his fancy.

Pop moved to Edmonds with us, leaving Nana and Letha at North Beach. He said it was to make sure that I wasn't neglected after the arrival of baby Alice. But I know he loved excitement and was drawn to the chaos of our young and vigorous family like a kid to a circus. Mostly occupied while his six children were growing up, ironically, at 80, he became a vivid and steady presence in our lives, for the next twenty-three years.

During the week, Dad was consumed by the Shop, so he was grateful for Pop's help. Pop felt useful and thrived on keeping busy. He watched over his wee charges, took care of the chickens, limed the fruit trees in spring, picked the fruit, and thinned the trees in fall. He bought and sold horses and fixed what needed to be fixed. For the next twelve years, Pop managed to keep Dad's rural estate fit and running.

Mom appreciated Pop's company and help around the farm, but his lumberjack cussing was not allowed around her little girls. He agreed, because Dad told him, "If you want to move in with us, you'll have to do whatever Pauline says." Mom's strict upbringing would not allow Pop to get away with anything crude. Once, he found a bottle of whiskey left by a road crew working near our Edmonds house. Alice saw him hide it and tattled. Mom made him throw it away. NO cussing and NO drinking. It must have galled Pop, but he kept the bargain.

Mom and Pop treated each other courteously. With her giving spirit, Mom welcomed him as part of the warm-hearted family she had never had; she honored him as Dad's father. He, however, was suspicious of her generosity and once asked, "Why are you so nice to me?"

"Because I love you, Pop," she said. He was unaccustomed to being lovable.

As it turned out, he was a gift. His agelessness was usual to us and contagious. A fit and youthful role model, we delighted in his lively attention and spirit. His rainbow of Mom-approved curses: "blue Moses;" "redheaded H;" "Nerts;" "blue pee-roo;" "Jesus, Mary, Joseph, and the apostles!;" "tarnation;" "perdition!," are childhood treasures, and his flamboyant descriptions, "smells like a hurrah's nest," "pusillanimous liar," "land o' Goshen!", "black-hearted reprobate," and "cussed fool!" are fond ghosts of the past. As young girls, we understood his anger was not intimidating, but creative.

He also shared his Chinese gambling lingo with a grin. "Mum-booee!-stop! Dimee peneshee!—give me the money! Kelu peneshee?—how much money? Lock sooee—rain! Ho hein—sunshine." It thrilled me to learn a "foreign language."

No stranger to providing fresh chicken for the dinner table, Pop was in charge of the henhouse in the barn. It had a small door leading to the chicken yard outside where the chickens and the rooster went in and out. I loved gathering the eggs, though it was scary in the smelly coop, scurrying by the unfriendly rooster, through the soiled straw to the nests, sometimes with a chicken sitting there. But, oh, what happiness to find a warm egg, or two, or three, and carefully place them in my basket. Best treasure hunt ever. I was a brave four-year-old, but not invincible.

"Nuh-huh, nuh-huh, nuh-huh." Me. Four. Crying.

"What's the matter? What happened? Pop.

"The Roo-ooster pecked me" Me. Crying.

"I'll fix that!" Pop walked toward the chicken coop. He came out holding the squawking rooster by the legs, put its head on the chopping block, chopped it off, and took the rest of the rooster in for dinner. My grandfather loved me.

Pop's great, stone grinding wheel was mesmerizing. He'd sit pumping pedals like a bicycle to get it whirling, sprinkle it with a little water, and lower a blade to its whizzing, gritty surface. He ground his tools razor-sharp, like the ax he used to chop off the rooster's head. I'd sit happily pedaling the stone wheel while Pop puttered in his shop. I'd pump and breathe in the heavenly smell of saddle soap and leather as he polished the horse harnesses on his workbench. He also had a treasure chest of saws, chisels, peelers, hand-cranked drills—I liked those best—handheld planers, rasps, hammers, a leather punch, and much more in his wooden toolbox. What a boon for me to learn the magic of tools from my grandpa.

I followed Pop wherever I could. One hot summer day, I watched him walk around the corner, and down the road toward town for Mr. Kouzmoff's funeral. I quickly put on my best white, rabbit-fur coat, and hustled my five-year-old legs after his unsuspecting figure. As I followed behind, the hot, summer sun beat down on my small figure, and I began to melt inside my fur coat. I had almost caught up when Mom came out of the house and called across the pastures for him to bring me back. He was late, we were too far toward town, so he motioned that he would take me with him. I beamed at my cunning.

Mr. Kouzmoff was the town's shoemaker, and the service was in the back of his darkened shop, where men in black suits—I don't recall any women—sat on folding chairs in the dim light. I sat on Pop's lap with my white fur coat brightening the atmosphere. My grandfather spoiled me.

Born in the 1865 horse-and-buggy era, working with and caring for horses was second nature. Pop loved their beauty, naming them, grooming them, employing their strength, and buying and selling them at the livery stable in Edmonds. At 85, he vigorously harnessed their energy to supply poles for fencing our acreage, logging a small patch of forest up Hummingbird Hill.

"Gee," he'd yell, and the team would go right. "Haw," he'd holler, and they'd move left. After felling the saplings, he'd tie the spicy, fresh-cut timber to the doubletree for the team to drag home. He taught me to use the peeler to strip the bark from the slender trees, leaving a long, golden pole for the fences.

Pop and Smokey

With Pop, I never felt afraid, even standing in a small stall beside a behemoth twice my height, cleaning the warm, sweet-smelling coat with a currycomb, then brushing the shining mane. Holding out my hand while a soft muzzle nibbled carrots or apples from my flat palm was never a fear, as Pop taught me how. I'd watch him work the horses in the pasture, holding a whip he never used. Smokey, Buck, Palo, or Tony, I never wanted for a horse to ride.

The year 1955 was big for the United States. Disneyland opened in California; Rosa Parks refused to give up her seat on the bus; the polio vaccine was declared safe; the first nuclear-powered submarine was launched; McDonald's built its first store; Coca Cola came out in cans; and my sister Robin was born. Another beautiful baby girl, but extra special for suffering jaundice and a damaged spleen.

Mom and Dad were relieved she had survived after the loss of two previous babies. A boy had strangled on the umbilical cord, and later, a girl, a "blue baby," had a congenital heart defect.

Thirteen years younger than I, Robin was like my own baby. Alice was 10 and Carol five, with a new baby sister. No longer the baby, Carol now felt the pinch of replacement. Pop was delighted to have another young one around. "Leave the baby be!" He'd bellow when we fussed over Robin too much and when Mom wasn't looking, he'd feed Robin butter from a table knife like he had with each of us when we were babies.

In Edmonds, Pop shepherded us little girls like kittens and he was happy to add another to his litter when Robin came. Alice, Carol, and I had spent wonderful years playing on the little farm on 9th Avenue in Edmonds. Robin spent only her toddler years there before we moved to Oz.

Dad took care of Pop, and Pop looked after us. Dad also took care of Nana and gave his sisters, Queenie, who had divorced, and Letha, who never married, jobs at his store so they had resources

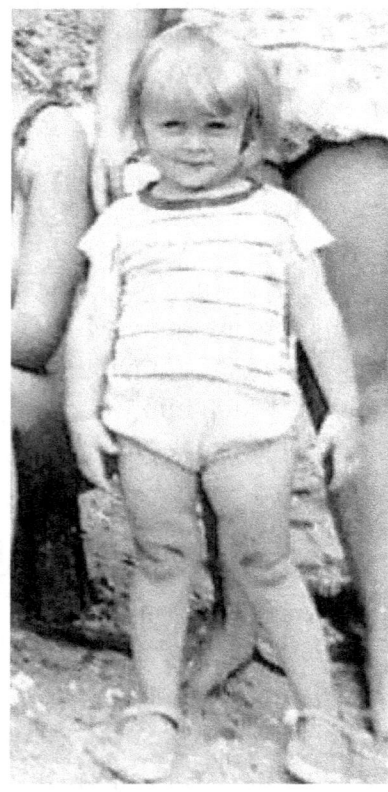

Robin Evonne Davison, 2

during the Great Depression and World War II. By 1946, at 34, Dad, the youngest in the family, had ferried twelve dependents through the tempests of the time. Sincere, reliable, good-hearted, and determined, he had no inkling that because of his responsible nature, stress and worry would later cause his life to drift away like an untethered skiff.

CHAPTER THIRTEEN
Windover Farm
1958—1995

The oppressive July heat pounded the roof of our Woodie station wagon, the air sweltering and still. We had been waiting in the car for hours! Hours to a kid, but probably about thirty minutes. "When are they coming back?" whined three-year-old Carol. "I think I'm getting heatstroke!" moaned Alice. "I'm tursty," whimpered Carol. We'd been playing in the opened back of the station wagon, parked in a dusty, unshaded, Montana parking lot, waiting for Mom and Dad who were in the real estate office. When they came back, we'd be going to look at another farm or ranch, but at least there would be wind while we drove.

Dad was born with itchy feet, and his travel trailer was the panacea. I was seven when our trailering began. Glacier National Park, Yellowstone, the Redwoods, and later, Disneyland were favorites. It was tedious each time we stopped at a real estate office to look at farm acreage. Washington, Oregon, California, Idaho, Montana, and

Polly, Alice, Carol, and Pauline Davison, 1950

Wyoming would produce a walnut farm, an avocado orchard, a cattle ranch, or other farm property. Dad was chasing the memory of his homestead childhood.

It took seven years of searching to find his dream in Central Washington, outside of Kittitas on the way to Badger Pocket, two hours east of Seattle. One hundred acres of fertile bottomland, with a two-story, four-bedroom farmhouse; two smaller houses; and outbuildings, including a barn, shop, chicken coop, granary, potato cellar, and an outdoor biffy. The works! In the fall of 1957, he bought it with ingenuity, using the Edmonds farm to accomplish the financing.

Dad's decision to move to Central Washington has left me with questions. Why wasn't he content with his small, five-acre farm? It had all the same bells and whistles, with much less labor. It was thirty minutes from work. We'd been part of the Edmonds community for thirteen years. Mom had found a house in a nice neighborhood of North Seattle near the Shop if we wanted to move, but Dad's desire for a large farm found us heading over the mountains to Oz. A respectful first child and fifteen years old, I never asked why.

The farm was called "Woodacres," after the previous owners, and renamed "Windover," by Auntie Queenie, referring to the valley's well-known breeze. In the middle of the school year, January 1958, gas cost thirty cents a gallon, Jerry Lee Lewis's "Great Balls of Fire" hit the top of the charts, and our family moved to the small town of Kittitas in Central Washington. I was a sophomore in a high-school class of 180 students, and excited about our new adventure, never considering that I might lose my childhood buddies

Windover—The Farm

from eleven school years in Edmonds. My twenty-five new sophomore classmates at Kittitas High School welcomed me graciously, and I took to them as fun new friends. Eventually, though, I lost contact with all but two of my early childhood chums. Time and distance cleared the field.

Occasionally, Alice and I would take the Greyhound bus for visits in Edmonds. The procedure was cringeworthy. Mom kept her watch set ten minutes ahead but still couldn't get anywhere on time. She'd pull up, blocking the bus moving out of the station, and run inside to buy our tickets. We'd board, heads bowed to avoid eye contact with faces of annoyed bus passengers. Mom would hurry back with the tickets, move the car, and off we'd go, hearts pounding as we sat beside some resentful soul, while Mom took her drama elsewhere.

I especially remember the smell of paint. The smell of new beginnings, exciting as well as terrifying. Each day after school, I'd get off the bus, stomp through the snow, and open the front door to paint fumes. After sixty years the smell of fresh, oil-based paint can instantly take me there. Remodeling had given the farmhouse an updated look; the woodwork was painted white; the old kitchen floor, countertops, and wallpaper replaced with bright, cacophonous orange and yellow coverings; living room carpet, orange and brown—a color pallet for the seventies, in 1958.

Renovation finished, Dad began commuting. He didn't worry about leaving us during the week because Pop was there. Dad had confidence in his father; there would be a man with Mom and his four daughters. Pop was 93.

On a snowy Monday morning, in the four o'clock

January darkness, Dad pulled away from the farm, beginning his two-hour drive to Ballard. The success of the Shop was important because of the family it took care of: Mom; my three sisters and me; Pop and Nana; his sisters, Queenie and Letha; and now, a hundred-acre farm.

Coming home, some Friday nights were rough. Two-lane U.S.10, snowstorms, accidents, or long backups at the North Bend stoplight during hunting season often extended his trip by hours. I can imagine his relief when out of the frigid darkness, he'd pull into the driveway, golden light shining from the farmhouse windows where Mom's hot beef stew and happiness were waiting for him.

I never understood why Dad didn't open a store in Ellensburg. There wasn't a floor-covering store in town, Letha and Queenie were capable of managing the Ballard store, and Mom could have managed a store close to home. Dad would have made calls, measured for jobs, ordered the materials for both stores, and he could have spent more time with us. When I asked, he said it wouldn't work. In retrospect, maybe there was more to it. We joke that Dad's slow-moving and deliberate nature couldn't keep up with Mom's constant energy.

> *Peter, Peter pumpkin eater*
> *had a wife and couldn't keep her*
> *Put her in a pumpkin shell*
> *and there he kept her very well.*

This repeated a family trait. Pop left Nana and his family on the Montana homestead to work in Glacier National Park; Dad was leaving Mom and us on the farm to work in Seattle. Mom was happy to help Dad realize his dream, and her pumpkin shell bloomed where it was planted.

Who would farm the one-hundred acres while Dad worked in Ballard? They found a reliable renter for the first several years. The second renter was not so dependable. He worked hard and paid the year's rent, but not the feed-store bill where he charged his seed, fertilizers, and supplies. At the end of the season, he took the alfalfa and left his debt to the landowners. The feed store let Mom work there to pay the debt down, and she also worked as a secretary at the Ellensburg Methodist Church to finish off the balance. After that debacle, the renters were chosen very carefully. Instead of alfalfa, cannery corn became the primary crop, and the new renter told Mom to take as much corn as she wanted. She was delirious with pleasure. Large ears of bright-yellow, fresh, juicy corn! As much as we could eat, whenever we wanted it. We were filled with the glory of corn. Enough to gorge and freeze, can, and give away to friends and family. Butter greased our chins from the end of summer into fall.

During our first years on the farm, Letha's old boyfriend, Don McDonald, died and left his estate to his aunt. He had always planned to outlive his aunt and live off her estate. Bad timing for both Don and Dad, as Dad was tapped out, having just bought the farm.

A call came from a lawyer inquiring about the quitclaim deed to Grapeview. The deed gave Dad ownership, but being the principled man he was, he wanted to pay something to the estate. He and the lawyer settled on $5,000. But Dad had no money. A friend offered a loan, but Dad turned him down in favor of sharing half ownership with his brother-in-law, Phil Schneider, his sister Phyllis' husband, in exchange for the $5,000.

Robert and Pauline, Phil and Phyllis drove from Seattle to Olympia to register the sale. Phil and Phyllis's grown children, Jean and Fred, came along. Mom and Dad were surprised when Phil, Jean, and Fred signed as owners with Dad and added the option for us girls to buy in for $1,000 at any time. We were too young and never able. The added owners worked out well, however, as Dad had help with the taxes and upkeep. Jean put the land into tree farm designation, lowering the taxes which she collected and paid each year. Now Grapeview belonged to us.

In the summer, while Mom was gone every day working hard to pay off the feed store bill, we girls were left alone, and mischief played. Nana and Auntie Letha would come to watch us—babysit. But when cousin Ginnie visited us for summer vacation, mischief reigned. Alice and Ginny were both 15 and trouble squared. They would smoke when no one was looking, steal alcohol used for cooking, and think up awful pranks. Their classic was the marshmallow caper.

Down the three stairs in the large kitchen pantry, Alice and Ginny giggled as Alice took the bag of large marshmallows from the upper shelf. She knew they were Robin's favorite. Handing the bag to Ginny, Alice took out a marshmallow and inserted a straight pin.

"Robin," they called, snickering, "Want a marshmallow?"

Five-year-old Robin came running, reached for the treat, and Alice stuck her arm.

"Ouch!" winced Robin, rubbing her skin.

"What?" Alice asked innocently.

"That hurt!" Robin frowned.

"No, it didn't," Ginny scoffed. "How could a marshmallow hurt you?"

"Ouch! She did it again."

Alice smirked.

"Auntie Letha, Alice is pricking me."

"She's just whining." Alice looked smug. "She's a whiny baby."

"Now, now girls." Auntie Letha came into the kitchen. "A marshmallow can't hurt you, sweet girl. Come and sit with me, Robin, and I'll read you a book."

Alice and Ginny smiled at each other and walked out of the pantry. Later that afternoon as Robin walked by the pantry again, Alice and Ginny burst out and stuck her with a marshmallow again. Poor Robin was defenseless until Mom came home and figured out what they had done. Punishment was applied but never enough for the trouble they caused.

Mom finally paid off the feedstore bill and decided to try growing alfalfa herself. One spring weekend, Dad seeded a sloping, eighteen-acre field. Through the summer, Mom and 14-year-old Carol pulled on their muck boots early in the fresh morning, walked to the alfalfa field, and set the irrigation ditch gate. It was tricky opening the gate just enough to soak the sloping field without wasting water. Then they walked home in the rising sun, Mom made breakfast, and worked in the garden or the house all day. After dinner, she and Carol donned their muck boots again, walked in the warm evening breeze back to the alfalfa field, closed the irrigation gate to stop the water and walked home in the setting sun. The alfalfa grew vibrant green and heavy in the 100° heat. After hard work and summer and fall cuttings, the crop made a little money, but not enough for the work it took.

Mom grew a large garden, canned fruit and vegetables, ground her own grain, and baked with it. She worked at church, played bridge with friends, sewed our clothes, and always had food for the rail-riding hobos who came to the back door. Her energy and love of farm life made it look easy. She helped in any way she could, with drama as her copilot.

It wasn't surprising that each time Mom took us to the bus station, she'd find someone in need: a woman in labor needing to go to the hospital; a runaway teenager who had changed his mind and needed a ride home; a man with a broken leg, unable to get to an appointment. She loved serving others. She'd solve the problem, then go home to finish her projects. Dad, in contrast, spent his days at the Shop and nights in a small trailer near his floor covering store. He'd heat soup on a propane burner for dinner, make calls, or write up orders in the evening until he could come home Friday night. Then he'd play catch up with family and farm work, unless it was too cold.

Winters on the farm were bright, snowy, and full of fun. Pop built a sleigh that Dad pulled behind the tractor. We'd bundle up in colorful coats, our noses frozen by the biting air, sitting on hay bales, gliding through the snow like kids a hundred years before.

Skiing was also a part of our winter sports growing up. Because Snoqualmie Pass was only forty-five minutes away, Mom would pack a picnic, and we'd hit the ski slopes for the day. Dad kept our leather boots oiled (before plastic polymer ski boots) and our skis waxed and with good cable bindings. Teaching us to ski was a big job for the only rooster in the hen house, but he tackled it happily, and with Mom's help, we learned and loved the skill.

After I married and moved away, Dad built an ice-skating rink in the yard, bought skates for Christmas, and Alice, Carol, and Robin practiced the spins and arabesques of skating champions. One very cold year in the 1980s, we were able to skate on the thick ice of a large field pond. With crackling flames of the bonfire at the pond's edge and double-bladed hockey skates on our feet, we flew in long strides over the frozen ice, cozy on the inside from effort, and icy on the outside from speed. Morrie, my husband, and I had five children by then and sharing this rare time with them is one of my fondest memories.

The farm was a blessing for Pop, and Pop was a blessing for the farm. He kept up repairs and tended the animals—things he'd done all his life. Because he couldn't drive, he'd sit on an apple crate beside the road and thumb rides to the nearby Clock Cafe. There, in his mid- nineties, he'd bet the passing truckers that they couldn't guess his age. He won a cup of coffee every time.

Buying and selling horses at the auction was his delight.

When Mom was busy, he'd thumb his way to Ellensburg. We teased him about the golden-haired lady he visited at the Ellensburg jewelry store. She sold him a beautiful necklace which he gave me for my engagement. He might have withered in Seattle, where his daughters wanted him to live, but active farm life kept him active and happy.

One afternoon when he was 94, he noticed a weasel in the front-yard oak tree. It was near dusk and he didn't want it to get away, so he hurried across the street, borrowed the neighbor's rifle, took careful aim in the dimming light, and hit the weasel with one shot! Another notch in his legend. Amazing really, since he hadn't touched a gun for decades.

Ten years on the farm and Mom's cheerful care gave Pop more time to live than most people, and my sisters and I were lucky to spend those last years with him.

Pop was chasing yearling calves in the barnyard one day when he had a stroke. He died several days later, six months short of his 103rd birthday. Robin came home from seventh grade to find him gone and was miserable that she hadn't said goodbye. Alice, Carol, and I, gone from home by then, said goodbye at his service, filled with family and friends who had enjoyed his colorful acquaintance. We granddaughters were infuriated when we discovered that someone at the funeral home clipped off the long, wicked, thumbnail on his left hand that he kept for fighting. He was buried beside Nana at Evergreen Washelli Cemetery in Seattle. I never think of him there. He lives in my memories.

Dad struggled with the Shop for the next several years and finally retired to the farm after we had all grown up. There, he made his fantasy into a country inn for family and friends. Carol's pals called it "Heaven Hotel." Mom and Dad welcomed everyone with big meals, sun-dried sheets, and home-made desserts. Thanksgiving, Christmas, and Easter were always busy, but Labor Day weekend, with the Ellensburg Rodeo, was the ultimate tradition. Tents, trailers, and a full house held rodeo revelers who came to celebrate the last weekend before the start of school.

In the shadows, however, feelings were hidden away.

Dad led us to Oz and then hid behind the curtain for fourteen years, visiting on weekends and trailer trips. He left Mom to battle hormonal and argumentative teenage daughters, trying to manipulate us from afar. His edicts, spouted from a gentler mouth, left us rebellious. With the enforcer away from home, why follow rules? I blamed Mom for the dysfunction until I realized that Dad was the puppeteer.

A traditional man with stubborn ideals, Dad built his cherished dream for his family. The irony was, in retrospect, it didn't fit. From the smart frock of a more contemporary suburban lifestyle in Edmonds, the farm felt like an ill-fitting dress to us girls. We tried to wear it for Dad's sake, but he left us. We tried to alter it in his absence but with lowered educational standards, and small-town thinking, the seams began to fray. The four of us acted out, frustrating and tricking sweet Mom who was happily oblivious to our unhappiness.

We loved it much more with the freedom of adulthood when it became a country haven for us and our children. Looking back, I'm glad Dad proved he could recreate his dream and share it with everyone. His dream brought him and Mom great happiness. He made a world of fun, supported by ingenuity, hard work, and travel.

On the other side of the coin, over the years, his ingenuity, hard work, and travel took its toll. Earlier stress and struggle to hold his two conflicting worlds together led to a breakdown he was careful to hide in plain sight.

CHAPTER FOURTEEN
Christmas Carol
1949—1972

Carol was born three days before Christmas, 1949. A tiny person from the beginning, Alice used her as a doll, dressing her up as a bride, a princess, or little Bunny Foo Foo for plays they put on.

We fondly remember our little, joyful toddler whose first sentence was "Ahm na gahdee." We were charmed but didn't know what it meant. "Ahm na gahdee," she'd say. "Ahm na gahdee." On the little farm there was a large vegetable garden where Mom worked each summer day. Finally, we realized

Carol Louise Davison

Carol was repeating Mom's parting call, "I'm in the garden."

Her first three years at Edmonds Elementary School found Carol the smallest in her class. When she moved to the farm in the middle of third grade, just after her ninth birthday, she met another small girl who became her partner at dancing lessons and her best friend. Lisa was the daughter of dance teacher, Lois Rahkonen. It's pleasant to remember the two little girls transformed into bouncing butterflies, antennae and wings flittering as they scampered and pirouetted across the stage. Lisa, who later became a renowned painter, captured their bright, colorful flight on canvas in a beautiful retrospect.

Carol didn't believe she was small. She was fierce, imaginative, and stood up for herself. Her big green eyes saw a happy world through which she skipped. But she wasn't perfect. Sibling rivalry often poked its devil's horns over her cherub face. Mom's job at the feed store, paying off the farmer's bill, left Carol and Robin home alone, and Carol, used that time to take revenge on her interloping little sister.

"Stop crying," Carol commanded. Robin's arms and legs flailed as she tried to jerk away to safety. Carol pinched Robin's nose shut tighter and adjusted her hand more firmly over Robin's mouth, but her five-year-old sister's wriggling broke her free, and she rolled away gasping for air. "I told you to stop crying," Carol said. "Now clean the bedroom, and I'll untie you when you're done." Five-year-old Robin tugged on the rope tied between her waist and the bedpost. It was just long enough to reach all corners of the room. She started to

tidy up the tossed clothing cluttering their shared bedroom. She couldn't wait to tell Mom when she came home.

"Oooooooh! Look out!" Carol whooped as her dishpan twisted and turned down the snowy hill toward Cousin Ginny. Alice, in her dishpan, sped by, as Lisa pushed off at the top of the hill. "My turn," Ginny shouted and ran to where Carol had stopped. Carol got out, and Ginny picked up the dishpan. I grabbed Alice's pan, and Ginny and I trudged up the hill. The falling feather flakes tickled my face. Each breath of frigid air shocked my warm lungs, and my nose felt icy, but the walk up the hill kept me toasty in my oversized snowsuit. For the next hour we took turns careening down the snowy slope, then plodded back to the cozy cabin. Dripping snowsuits hung from nails in the mudroom as we sopped up chicken stew with Mom's fresh

Cousin Ginny Miller with Carol Davison

Cabin at Snoqualmie Summit

biscuits. A promise of brownies drifted from the woodstove oven.

The cabin was Dad's treat for us, built on property in the Cascade Mountains, sometime in the mid-fifties after Robin was born. He didn't realize at the time that it would serve two purposes. Dad and Pop constructed the cabin in sections on the farm in Edmonds, trailered the sections to Snoqualmie Summit and put the cabin together there. Dad was a visionary. Prefabricating a building, done only in the military at that time, was a rare technique for the 1950s. It became big business years later. He made the roof of corrugated tin panels, innovative for mountain cabins in those days, so the heavy snow would slide off. When the cabin was done, it was another happy place Dad made for his family.

In winter, we sisters tumbled in the deep, white fluff,

and delighted in skiing, sledding, and bringing friends to play in the snowdrifts, sometimes twelve feet deep, enough to reach up to the second-floor cabin door. In summer, the woods were fragrant with cedar, blackberry, and woodsy spices enhanced by the heat. A stream behind the cabin ran cold and clear and was our water source. We would invite friends and run the woods like native creatures, then come in for berry pie, which Mom baked from the huckleberries we picked on bushes around the cabin. Carol's love for the outdoors started there, as she and Lisa played through the seasons.

Things took a tumble for Carol in fifth grade and kept on rolling. At ten years old, as usual, she was still the most petite person in her class.

During an annual checkup, her doctor, an overzealous country practitioner—Alice called him a duck, meaning a quack—scared Mom and Dad with the word *dwarfism*. Dad's anxiety triggered and Mom took Carol to be studied at the University of Washington Medical Center for a week of blood tests, brain tests—brain scans were not in use until later—X-rays, and painful, intrusive probing. Dad's belief in the power of medicine, formed when he was young, kept him from shielding Carol from the poking, prodding, and humiliation. Mom mirrored Dad, so Carol was handed over for several weeks of medical research.

"Mom, I don't want to do this anymore." Carol's eyes flashed with revolt. "I'm done with needlesticks and band-aids. I hate these dumb hospital gowns, and I hate when the doctors talk about my private parts. It's been too embarrassing."

"I'm sorry, Sweetie. The tests are almost finished,"

Mom answered.

"You've said that before. Yesterday they really hurt me, Mom. My arm is black and blue where the nurse stabbed the needle." Carol scooted off the examination table and rolled up her sleeve to show the dark bruise. "This hospital stuff is creepy."

"They just want to be sure you're healthy. We'll get ice cream when you're done today."

"I *am* healthy. This is stupid." Carol's voice dropped to begging. "Please, can't I stop?"

"Your daddy wants to know what the doctors find out. He wants you to finish the tests. I think they'll be done tomorrow, and we can go home."

With the back of her hand, Carol wiped the moisture from her eyes.

Carol Davison, 11

When the doctors finished their studies, she was found to be... perfectly healthy. Just a lovely, petite girl. Mom was five foot, four inches tall and Dad was five-foot-six. What was so hard to figure?

Dad's worry hung over us precariously throughout our lives. We were caught off guard each time it descended, changing our worlds. Carol experienced this anxiety firsthand, and her faith in him was jarred. He loved us totally; he worked hard to give us a beautiful life, but his anxious nature undermined our trust.

The Shop had financial trouble in 1962 and Mom was needed to help. Carol was entering sixth grade and her teenage years when she and Robin were transferred from Kittitas Grade School to Ballard Elementary for the year. The four lived in a small rental house and came home on the weekends. With the move and stress of an unsettled family, she did not do well. Carol, as a thirteen-year-old nomad, became rebellious with hormones, and resentment from the hospital torture. Her funny, creative and outgoing personality that would shine later in life, shriveled in Ballard. She could be cruel and oftentimes Robin was the goat.

The lights flashed on. "FIRE! FIRE! Get up! Hurry! Get outside!" Carol yelled, holding a pan of smoking paper.

Seven-year-old Robin and her cousin Jay awoke groggily from their sleepover on the living room pull-out-couch, and hurried outside, gingerly stepping onto the cold cement porch. Icy winter wind tore through their thin nightclothes when they heard the front door lock.

In the house, Carol doused the burning paper in the sink. She and Sandra, Jay's older sister, searched and found their siblings' underwear and hung the unmentionables over surrounding lampshades. Giggling at their mischief, they unlocked the front door and let the shivering children in. Mom and Dad were awake by then, and angrily grounded Carol. I'm sure Robin would have increased the punishment.

The year in Ballard was a trial for Mom and Dad, a trial

for Carol and Robin, and on the farm, a disconcerting time for Alice and me.

While the rest of the family lived in Ballard, we were left in Kittitas with Pop. I'm not sure who was watching whom. Pop was 97. Nana and Auntie Letha visited occasionally, and I went to Central Washington State College in Ellensburg and lived at home. It was a time of freedom for me. Little parenting and college fun.

But when roused, Dad's reach was far. During the family absence I worked at the Liberty Theater, the only theater in Ellensburg, to pay my college tuition by spending my evenings at the theater and attending classes during the day. It sure beat my last job standing on the back of a potato digger removing rocks from the potatoes coming up from the ground onto a belt.

I loved my work greeting happy people at the ticket window, selling popcorn at the snack bar, and walking the aisles with my flashlight to discourage hanky-panky. Sometimes I helped at the summer drive-in theater.

I'd worked at the Liberty for more than a year when a movie titled "The Naked Virgins" came to the family theater. Though a titillating title to lure in college students, it was a National Geographic-like documentary about tribal Africa.

Just before the movie's run was over, the manager came up to me and said, "I'm sorry, but you can't work here anymore. I have to let you go."

Dumbstruck, I said, "I don't understand."

"Your father has written us a letter, and we have no choice," he said kindly.

I was blindsided. Dad had said nothing to me about

any letter. Apparently he was unhappy about the title "The Naked Virgins," and, never having seen the movie, decided that I shouldn't work there. Instead of talking with me, he made his wishes known from Ballard in a letter to the theater. I felt betrayed. What other job would balance as well with my studies?

When he wasn't roused, his complicated life left us on our own.

Alice was a frisky senior in high school, and with parents away, suffered from rumors and a false, small-town reputation which turned into embarrassment for Carol. On a Girl Scout Camping trip, she was humiliated to overhear two leaders discussing what a tramp her sister Alice was. Distressed, Carol repeated this to Alice who went straight to the offending adult, threatening a lawsuit if the woman didn't stop the gossip. With Mom and Dad away, Alice learned to take care of problems herself.

The Shop survived and the family was back together when school started in the fall of 1963. A year had passed, and we girls had grown. Dad tried harder to control us but, as happens, couldn't put the toothpaste back in the tube.

Carol's next few years were fraught with trouble. Mom, with too much on her plate, and unsettled by Carol's rebellion, did not pay enough attention to school.

Seventh grade was not easy for Carol. Her teacher, Mrs. Grant, had a reputation for being strict. She turned out to be a nightmare. Carol felt her dislike and seventh grade became another unhappy year in a negative rut and digging.

"Your penmanship is sloppy. Do it over."

"Get the gum out of your mouth, and go stand in the

garbage can with your nose touching the wall."

"No. You can't go to the restroom until recess!"

Carol persevered but the deep hurt Mrs. Grant inflicted, fueled the flames of her increasing anger.

Between Carol's seventh and eighth grade years in 1964, the spotlight was mine. I graduated from college, became Mrs. Morris Pedersen, and went off to become a teacher.

Just before ninth grade, Carol, at 14, ran away to Seattle. Mom blocked her way and Carol threw her into the kitchen sink. I tried to stop her—I was seven months pregnant—and she pushed me down in the driveway. Off to Ellensburg she flew, hopped on a bus, and headed for Seattle. Dad sped from Ballard to Snoqualmie Summit, took her off the bus, and brought her home. So much drama. If she was looking for attention, she got it. But I think Carol was searching for peace and consistency.

Sullen rebellion haunted her high school years, and in April 1968, just before graduation, Pop died, leaving her more miserable, with a large hole in her heart. The farm, an elixir for Dad, was a bitter pill for Carol.

Graduation in June saw her bolt across the mountains to Seattle and move in with Cousin Sandy, a surprise for Sandy's mom. Jean welcomed Carol—with Mom's blessing—and rearranged Sandy's room for two. As the trees brightened with orange and gold in September, Carol enrolled in nearby Shoreline Community College, while Sandy began her senior year of high school. With liberty, came a freed spirit. Carol flourished. She chose recreation as her major, tried out for plays, and found lifelong friends in the theater department. Freedom dissolved

Graduation Photo—Carol Davison, 18

her rebellion.

The top was down on the little, bright yellow VW convertible when it stopped in our driveway. Out hopped Auntie Carol, wearing a dormouse costume and carrying a rainbow of colored balloons for niece Amie's seventh birthday. That was the essence of Carol. No longer the tortured teenage soul, but a colorful and blithe spirit, hidden away, now ready for fun.

Carol's abrupt exit and Pop's death left only Robin and Mom on the farm. I was married with two children, Alice was away at college. Without Pop, the farm was a lonely place for Mom. Dad, tired of living in a trailer, was delighted when she and Robin came back across the mountains and rented a small apartment in north Seattle near Carol. Robin transferred from Kittitas to Shoreline, for eighth grade. When the apartment grew too small Dad bought a split-level house in Robin's Shoreline school district. In Kittitas, the farmhouse became a rental. When she felt the parental harness was removed, Carol started working at the Shop to pay for school, and to Mom's relief, moved back in with the family. Carol finished her AA degree at Shoreline Community College as Alice graduated from Western Washington State College in Bellingham.

Dad thought this an excellent reason to celebrate his smart daughters with a six-week trailer trip across the western United States. He, Mom, Alice, Carol and Robin aimed for the great national parks: Yosemite in California; Yellowstone in Wyoming; Glacier in Montana; Bryce Canyon, Zion, and Arches in Utah; and anywhere else they chose to go —Disneyland was on the list. They ran free, tethered only to their imaginations. Through hot, piney forests; deep, shadowy canyons; or deserts swept by broiling wind, Alice, Carol, and Robin sat in the back seat of trailer-pulling "Fishtail," a 1960 Ford station wagon that swayed in the rear end. With the windows down, they sat wearing bathing suits, their skin smeared in cocoa butter, hoping for a tan.

Six weeks later Dad pulled into the driveway of their Seattle house. They all began to unpack, but he couldn't stand it. "Let's go to the ocean," he said.

Alice and Carol Davison

Mom loaded in a few fresh supplies and off they went for several more days of salty beach time. Dad hated to come back to life's traces.

With her AA degree in recreation completed, Carol returned from vacation to a job with the Seattle Parks Department as a specialist in senior citizen activities. Growing up with Pop had taught Carol that age wasn't counted in years but in spirit. Leading lively day trips and tours around King County was a perfect fit. She loved her seniors, and fondly called them her "raisins."

CHAPTER FIFTEEN
Rough Rapids
1972—1988

Imagine sunning at the beach. A call for help sends you into the water. While you're trying to assist, the incoming tide quietly floats your belongings away. That was how it was when Dad drifted off. We were all distracted by Carol's trouble.

1978 was the momentous year Mom and Dad retired to the farm. Carol quit her job with the Seattle Parks Department and came along. Finishing her BA in Recreation at nearby Central Washington State College, the four-foot, eleven inch fireball used her degree to guide outdoor

Carol Davison

hikes and camping trips throughout the Pacific Northwest. She spent one winter teaching skiing on the slopes near Whitefish, Montana. The following summer she stayed to guide backpackers in surrounding grizzly bear country, wearing bells on her backpack and hanging supplies from trees overnight to keep the bears away.

Back home again, the farm became home base while she led camping trips through the Washington mountains and rafting trips on Northwest rivers.

Her favorite outdoor activity, though, was the "invitation only" Gourmet River Float each summer on the Yakima River. Dining on fine china and silver while inner tubing through the Kittitas Valley with a group of college friends, leaves me wondering what ended up on the bottom of the river.

While Carol romped through the Pacific Northwest, Mom and Dad were busy traveling or working to keep the farm a showpiece.

The large, green lawn that surrounded the farmhouse took a lot of care. Mom decided to help using the riding lawn mower. Dad checked the gas, taught her about the controls, and off Mom went, her white sweater flapping in the breeze. He worked in the carpenter shop, half listening to the motor's hum until there was silence. He heard Mom hollering, "Help! Help!" and took off running, fearing the worst. As he came around a corner, he saw the lawnmower turned on its side, Mom's legs kicking out from underneath. He grimly righted the machine and Mom crawled out.

"I got warm so I took my sweater off and hung it over the back of my seat, " Mom explained. "It must have slipped down and gotten snarled in the motor. Next thing I knew, the darn thing started to tip, and over I went. I'm so glad you heard me. I seemed to be under there forever."

Dad shook his head and helped Mom up. As soon as his heart had stopped pounding and Mom had gone into the house, he began to pull the strands of wool out of the engine, piece by piece. Pauline always made life exciting.

Vacations at the summit were long gone by the mid-seventies and the property was put on the market. That's when Dad's recycling skill became epic. The buyers decided they didn't want the cabin; they said that Dad could have it, probably thinking it impossible to move—a miscalculation. On a summer weekend, before the sale was final, Dad gathered a crew and deconstructed the prefabricated cabin, trailered the sections to Grapeview, and rebuilt it there, near the beach. He laughed to himself, thinking of the buyer hunting the property for the building after the escrow closed.

The cabin at Grapeview gave us independence. Over the years our Dad's sister Phyllis and her two grown children had built three bungalows on the ridge above the waterfront, and now we had our own; no need to stay in the old house or with anyone else. The cabin had two floors, like at the summit, and was just as rudimentary. On one end of the rectangular first level, Mom and Dad's bedroom was behind the stairs, next to the front door. The rest of the main floor was open. The cabin's big wood-burning cookstove, perpendicular to a sidewall, sat near a plywood counter with a sink for washing dishes in water carried from the old well. There was no drain; dirty dishwater was thrown on the bushes outside the door. On the opposite end of the main floor mismatched easy chairs, rocking chairs, and sofas filled the space, with a grand, round, oak table for meals, and a deck outside sliding doors. The walls were unfinished. Vertical bats of foil-covered insulation ran from floor to ceiling, covering the wood between the studs and shining with reflective light. Mom didn't mind the unfinished atmosphere. She loved people, not decor.

Under a tall, peaked roof, the second floor could accommodate a crowd of family and friends, happy to be together except on baked beans night. Windows at each end, the large open space was furnished with bunk beds sporting mattresses filled with straw. I can remember mornings on a hard straw mattress, waking to the delicious smell of bacon, coffee, and beach. To save us the long, dark, walk to the outhouse at night, Dad placed a chamber pot at the top of the stairs.

Living at Grapeview was primitive, but with a roof, a wood stove, water, and electricity, we were satisfied. Mom made it wonderful with love, great cooking, and hard work. She was also a Master of Games, winning most of the games she played. Carol loved Grapeview, her personal playground full of water fun and lazy comfort. She shared the magic with her friends who came to swim, pick oysters, row the boat to Harstine Island, eat steamed clams fresh from the beach, or play "Pig," Mom's favorite card game, at the big, round, oak table on rainy days. She treasured Grapeview and carried it in her heart.

In 1983, Carol found her dream job. She was 34, living on the farm with Mom and Dad. Madigan Air Force Base near Tacoma, Washington, advertised for a civilian recreation director. It was an ideal situation. Interviewed

Carol Davison

and hired, she put her creativity to work, planning recreational activities on base, and producing traveling entertainment for other military installations. The Air Force talent surprised her. Great singers, dancers, actors, and band members promised quality extravaganzas and sparked her inventiveness and energy. She moved near the base to a small apartment, with ceilings so low she called it her "Pygmy Palace," and started her professional career with a place of her own and a job that fired her enthusiasm. Her performances were dazzling and toured internationally. The recreation activities she planned, to Northwest Trek, skiing, or to the ocean, were welcomed on base. She loved her work.

Her production for bases in Germany was ready to go in 1985 when she went for a required medical check-up before she could leave the country. There was a spot on her cervix. The biopsy showed cancer. A maelstrom of tests and doctors' visits followed. She wasn't married or with children; she had only Mom and Dad to hold on to, so they became her anchors. It was heartbreaking for both of them but, Mom, the "Energizer Bunny," met the diagnosis with strength, while it lay on Dad's heart like a ponderous stone.

Dad, with a fundamental Christian soul, read the scriptures literally. He felt responsible for Carol's illness, believing the "sins of the father," meant sins were passed on from one generation to the next, and he felt guilty. An inborn fear of sinfulness in himself and by extension, in us, provoked his constant fight for control. He pictured us drawn to darkness rather than light. But his belief in Jesus was profound so he also felt certain Carol could be healed through the light of Christ.

Carol wrestled with chemo and radiation. When she lost her hair, she bought a bright red wig and, laughing with her zany chums, became 'Flame La'fleur,' party girl extraordinaire. Eventually, the treatment worked, and she was pronounced "in remission," to everyone's relief.

Her job at Madigan continued to bring joy for the next couple of years as she continued staging entertainment with the talented personnel on base. Some sang, some danced, some played in the band or acted in skits. Shaping the talent and traveling to other Air Force bases made her feel alive with artistry. She bought a small house in Tacoma, which we helped paper, paint, and personalize. The backyard was a cluster of color collated by the previous owner. Framed against the dark green firs of the Pacific Northwest, the spring provided rhododendrons in ruby hues, yellow narcissus and daffodils, purple lilacs, snowy magnolia, pink dogwood, and rosy-hued camellias.

Summer and fall popped with daisies, asters, a myriad of colorful roses sunning against the house, dahlias, black-eyed Susans and more; and in the back corner, under the trees, native trilliums lovingly transplanted from the wild. It was a breathing space for the soul.

Carol loved parties. Her little house vibrated with celebrations year-round, and each October brought cider pressing in the backyard, with press and apples from the farm. Family, old friends, and new friends from Madigan filled the yard with cups of tangy cider and laughter.

We lived in Gig Harbor at that time and having Carol nearby was new. I hadn't seen her as much since we were children. She came to picnics, school baseball games, dance recitals, and choir concerts. Her nieces and nephews were

Carol's Air Force Entertainment Group

blessed to have her around. She would meet Morrie and me once a week for cheap movies. We took good advantage of our time together.

One evening in 1987 the phone rang.

"Pauli!" Carol's voice was crying. "I have an awful pain in my leg," she moaned as another spasm stabbed her. "I don't think I can drive to the hospital."

"I'll be right there." I grabbed my keys and got to her in ten minutes.

At the hospital, they relieved her pain but found that her cancer had returned.

Carol didn't want surgery, "to be carved up piece by piece." Instead, she followed the doctor's chemical regimen while trying other remedies: Indian spirit healing, Japanese Reiki, a procedure in Mexico, a miso diet. Nothing could halt the cancer.

As Carol fought with cervical cancer, aunts, uncles, and cousins, in contention, decided to sell Grapeview. Carol told Dad that if he agreed to the sale, it would kill her. Dad's no vote was in the minority, so the place of our hearts for over a half-century was put on the market. Dad's heart surely broke. He would have done anything to help her, but he didn't have the power to save Grapeview. Unrecognized until later, his failure to heal Carol and keep Grapeview from being sold pushed him beyond his mental limit.

Easter morning was cold. It was 1988 and the Kittitas Baptist Church was holding Sunrise Service on the front lawn of Windover Farm. As the sun rose over the congregation of chilly churchgoers, a crowd of curious cows stood watching from the other side of the fence. They seemed to enjoy the service, too, but missed the following pancake breakfast.

Later, our family gathered for the children's Easter egg hunt, and the highly anticipated Easter feast: ham, scalloped potatoes, green beans, broccoli, marshmallow salad, deviled eggs, Caesar salad, olives, Auntie Letha's Jello salad, Mom's pies, and pies, and pies, and pies! Everyone ate as much food as they could. It was an insult not to go back for seconds!

We were dozing in the living room in food comas when Dad brought out a bottle of olive oil. He wanted to perform the ritual "laying on of hands" by the elders (James, 5:14) and anoint Carol's head with oil. Painful awkwardness sucked air from the room. His misery was so great, and his Christian need to heal his daughter so strong, that her embarrassment and humiliation mattered little to him. She turned her back and went upstairs, his desperation undermining her hope.

Like before, Mom stuck to Carol like Super Glue. At appointments, procedures, and consultations, including a trip to Mexico, Mom's optimistic spirit was at Carol's side. As time passed, Mom's memory began to fail, and we worried that she was getting Alzheimer's. But it was emotional stress as Carol just kept wearing away, becoming thinner and thinner. The drugs for her pain left her groggy. She quit her job as the cancer became worse. She was still Carol, but drugs made her hazier. The summer passed. Finally, Mom and Dad came over the mountains to stay at her house. We all surrounded her with love.

At the end of September, in the hospital, she mostly slept. "I'm a child of the sixties," she said, "give me drugs." The drugs kept her lingering.

"Don't worry," we said. "Go when you're ready."

As the week went by she'd wake and ask, "Am I dead yet?"

"Nope, not yet," we'd answer.

Carol passed away on a brilliant orange and gold October day. As I walked out of the hospital into warm autumn sunshine I was glad that her suffering was over. Physically gone, she's never left our hearts. I think Dad's heart shattered that day. His faith was shaken, and something shifted in his already delicate brain.

On a current of grief, he surged out of the shallows and into the mainstream, moving more swiftly on the long, winding river.

CHAPTER SIXTEEN
Changes
1995

Dear Father in Heaven,
Thank you for this beautiful day and the blessings you bring.

I need your help. Bob's anger and discontent with me are hard to bear. His sweet and loving personality is disappearing, and his accusations and meanness are painful. This isn't like him. I'm so sorry for his unhappiness and confusion. Please help me to soothe his dissatisfied spirit.

Help him to find his way back home when he goes into town. Help him to know how much I love him, and that I'm not his enemy. Help him to sleep through the night without wandering. Help him not to lose the dear heart he's always had. And help me to carry him through this trouble. Through Jesus Christ, I pray, amen.

Mom rose from her knees and went to make Dad's breakfast. Always a positive presence in our lives, Mom was sweet, kind, funny, and giving. She was Dad's sidekick and a firm deputy to his role as sheriff in our lives. A role model of the fifties, her faith, and her upbringing, Mom respected Dad's thinking and took it for her own. She followed him in every way: politics, culture, nutrition, child-rearing, recreation, religion. In her eyes, he could do no wrong. Because Mom happily accepted Dad's changing behaviors, we were slow to throw the life ring when he was drowning. His Christian passion and complex personality made it often difficult to tell whether he was eccentric or daft.

In 1947, as the Polaroid camera came on the market, I turned five. That summer, Mom helped me pack my suitcase for a trip the next day to visit Uncle Paul in California. In the morning, ready to go, Dad decided to varnish our Woodie station wagon. He slowly and meticulously scraped, sanded, and applied the strong-smelling varnish. Three days later, when the wood was dry, we hit the road. In those days his quirkiness was considered amusing.

Dad was a character. He was a dreamer who made his homestead fantasies into real life. Love and family loyalty ran deeply in his character. A sense of humor hid his urge to control, and Christian judgment propelled his actions. His logic was tricky to understand and his actions were often puzzling. As life went on, we became used to his idiosyncrasies, and when they turned south, we weren't watching.

Grapeview proved an interesting problem in the early eighties. Dad was worried about thieves getting into the cabins through the long, private track from the road, so he added more chains and more locks to the gates until he had a good collection of necessary keys. This worked as long as he gave new keys to the other families who had cabins there, but that didn't always happen. One of the families would arrive after the two-hour drive, car packed for a week's stay, and find the gate chained with a new padlock. This happened more than once. The quarter mile walk through the shaded track to the cabin was beautiful, but not while lugging your gear for a long stay. Luckily there was a back way a mile down the road. Was this obsession normal, or part of his impending brain skew?

During those same years, his love of God took on stronger and stronger intensity which eventually led to friction with his church. Was this a precursor of trouble ahead or normal zeal? His actions were repeatedly confusing.

Grandson Chris was ten when he began spending summer vacations on the farm. Farming was in his blood, and Grandpa Robert and Grandma Pauline welcomed him to experience an agricultural life and help Grandpa with chores. Chris loved his Grandpa and spent six summers in the early eighties in rural ecstasy. He learned good habits: how to take care of tools and machinery; how to chop wood and store it for the winter; and how to drive the tractor. He had freedom to take the moped scooter whenever and wherever he chose, mostly fishing at the big irrigation ditch on the hill.

He became familiar with stories about his great-grandfather, Pop; gathered nuggets of wisdom from Grandpa Robert; and attended Vacation Bible School at his grandpa's church. The dark side of religion emerged the summer of Chris' twelfth birthday when Grandpa Robert and adult cousin Randy introduced him to heaven.

Chris reached down and scratched the silky ears of the small, brown barn kitten. It always ran to him when he entered the yard. Neighbor Scotty Brown sat on the overwintered combine they would use today for the first hay cutting of the season. He tested the hydraulics on the cutter bar and rotating rake, then swung the side auger out and flipped on its switch. A slow grinding sound emitted as it started to turn, and black and white debris of baby starlings shot out and landed flapping on the ground. Scotty's four-year-old son, who was scampering through the rusted plows and harrows in the side lot, ran over and began to stomp them, delighted. Scotty got down to help his son, and said to Chris, who was looking pale, "This is just the way a farm runs, Chris. Those dang buggers make a dirty mess wherever they go. Better to get rid of them while they're young." Chris felt his stomach turn over. "Hop on the combine and we'll head for the fields."

He jumped up the steps to the cab as Scotty backed the cumbersome machine toward the barn, then slowly pulled ahead, turning the big rig toward the gate. As Chris watched the receding barnyard, he saw the dead barn kitten, lying in the dirt, accidentally flattened by the backing combine. That evening, Chris, his heart hurting about what had happened earlier in the day, said, "Grandpa, what happens when you die?"

Grandpa Robert saw this as a perfect opportunity to school his young grandson on the realities of becoming a godly man.

"Well," answered his Grandpa, "you have to be born again in Jesus, and then you go to heaven."

"Do animals go to heaven?"

"No. The only way to get there is through Jesus. I love you and want you to understand about Satan and the trouble he'll cause if you don't know Jesus," Grandpa said.

"I know Jesus, Grandpa, he's always been in my heart."

"We're all evil, and born sinners," Grandpa Robert testified. "The devil's waiting to trick you. If you're on his side, you'll never see your mama, or daddy, or any of your family again; you'll be left, alone, when we go to heaven. You've got to fear the Lord," Grandpa Robert said. "The only way out is to take Jesus as your Lord and Savior and be born again."

Chris felt the pressure of tears behind his eyes. "I don't fear Him Grandpa; I love Him. I was already born in Him." Why was Grandpa trying to destroy a feeling that was so precious and wonderful, Chris thought.

"You're a sinner," Cousin Randy said, "you were born that way. Your grandpa and grandma take you in each summer because your parents can't handle you."

Terrorized, Chris spoke their words and spent the rest of the night frightened and in tears, afraid of losing his family, and grieving the dead. In religious zeal, Dad gave his trusting young grandson nightmares for years to come. When Chris told his grandma the next morning, she said, "Oh, they did that to Auntie Robin, too."

My mom, Pauline, was the maker of pies, soother of ills, servant of God, lover of chocolate, knitter of sweaters, reader of fairy tales, winner of games, tireless worker, and disciple of Dad. She loved their life and followed him without question. When Dad's transformations started at *the end of the eighties, Mom kept them to herself.*

We overlooked the empty eyes of his fiftieth-anniversary photo in 1989. We overlooked his jealousy of Robin's new baby, born in 1993. His growing desire to spend money, to eat out every night, to tell the same old stories, as well as his frailty and confusion, Mom swept aside out of loyalty. Because of her strange childhood, her faithfulness to Dad was rock solid.

His transformation remained opaque until I found bananas in the guest room closet and had to admit something significant was happening.

"Do you smell bananas?" I asked Morrie, outside our guest bedroom in February of 1995.

"Yeah. I've been smelling bananas here ever since your Mom and Dad left. The smell's getting stronger."

I poked around in the guest room closet, wrestled through the hanging winter clothes, and there were two, overripe bananas placed carefully on the floor at the back. There was the proof, Dad was seriously off. But this was nothing compared to the "money laundering."

CHAPTER SEVENTEEN
Money Laundering
Spring 1995

Sudsy, hot water slopped over the edge of the basin onto the plywood surface. Scooping a handful of gritty silver coins, Robin tossed them, clinking to the bottom, picked up the washcloth, and scrubbed a dime between her cloth fingers.

Dad's hidden skeletons began to slip from the closet in the early 1990s. He was nearly 80. Mom caught on early, and smoothly covered his awkward forgetfulness, confusion, or paranoia. Distracted by my young family, I missed the signs. When he spilled his tea on our visit to Mom's Theda relatives, I wondered why he was so overwhelmingly embarrassed, out of proportion with an ordinary mishap—it was just an accident.

Then, one morning in the spring of 1995, Dad called and a skeleton hit me on its way out of the closet.

"Pauli, you have to come and help your mom!" His voice was raspy, exasperated. The call was strange. Mom was the communicator; Dad had never phoned me before.

"What does she need, Dad?"

"The dimes and quarters are slippery, and her hands can't pick them up. She needs help."

I raked my memory for a smidgen of understanding, but nothing came to explain his distress.

"Sure, Dad, I'll be there as soon as I can." I was clueless. I phoned my younger sister Alice who had worked at the store with Dad for many years. She and my sister Robin, thirteen years younger, knew what I didn't. Dad had buried money on the farm around 1975. He was digging it up.

While I was raising five young children in the 1970s, Richard Nixon, Gerald Ford and Jimmy Carter paraded past as presidents. None a smashing success. Gratefully, the Vietnam War ended, and Title IX was passed for funding girls sports, but the decade was a time of great political, cultural, and economic turmoil. Inflation and interest rates rocketed to the sky, which left me struggling to pay for basics, like fresh food, toothpaste, and shoes. To fill our gas tanks then, during the Arab oil embargo, we parked our car overnight in a long line to the gas station.

Financial guru Howard Ruff took advantage of the 1970's stormy financial seas by frightening readers of his newsletter *Ruff Times,* to which Dad subscribed. Ruff fished with survivalist bait. His books, *Famine and Survival in America*, 1974, and later, *How to Prosper During the Coming Bad Years,* 1979, warned of hard times ahead. Having survived the Great Depression, Dad's worry gene made him an easy catch. He lived by the Boy Scout motto "be prepared." Ruff's newsletter predicted that the United States was headed for "hyperinflationary economic depression," and that everyone should store a year's supply of food and buy "junk silver" as protection from unrest in the cities. Dad's anxiety propelled him. He contacted Howard Ruff's organization and bought $20,000 of junk silver coins to use if the government collapsed, and enough preserved survival food packages to last a year. Taking good care of his family was always a priority.

What is "junk silver?" It's used silver coins, pulled from circulation by the United States, Canada, Australia, or the United Kingdom when one-third of its worth has been rubbed off. Its face value no longer counts, only its weight. Dad's junk silver was made up of US dimes, quarters, and half-dollars, which arrived in canvas bags. The idea was to use the devalued coins for food, shelter, gas, and necessities during the coming times of social calamity. In 1975, Dad received $20,000 in junk silver, but never verified the weight. He dug a pit in an old garage on the farm in Central Washington, dropped the canvas bags and his coffee cans of loose change into the hole, packed dirt on top, then parked there regularly. The survival food packages were stored in a guest house. If a panic occurred, he was ready. Fifty years later, it did come, but too late to use Dad's supplies.

Happy years passed on the farm from the seventies through the eighties and five years into the nineties when Dad tripped over a cat on the farmhouse lawn. A few months later, he was hospitalized with an enlarged heart, and the doctors found he'd recently suffered a stroke—the stroke, not the cat, caused his fall. Dad, hiding his failings over the last few years, dreaded the time he'd have to sell the farm. He knew that time was now, before the creeping darkness took over his ability to think. With fading canniness, he bought Mom a new, purple—her favorite color—Dodge Caravan to use after his memory was gone. And he proceeded to dig up the buried treasure.

As a dim bulb dangled from the roof of the wooden garage, doing little to illuminate the digging site, Dad pulled bags from the shoveled ground, and the rotted canvas ripped apart, spilling coins over greasy dirt. Mom's gnarled, arthritic hands could hardly pick them up. Dad was beside himself, so he called me, the oldest daughter, forgetting he'd never let me in on the secret.

Mom and Dad were in the old garage when my sisters and I pulled into the farm in Central Washington, just outside Kittitas. Dimes, quarters, and half dollars scattered across the earth and oil of eons, winking dully in the low light of the garage. I sniffed the bitterness of mildew and moldering soil.

Every summer, commercial crops in the Kittitas Valley are irrigated by lakes in the Cascade Mountains. The water table in the valley fluctuates, so the groundwater under the garage rose and fell over the years, rotting the canvas bags. It was a grimy mess and took us the rest of the day to gather all of the coins and clean up. That evening we made plans. On our trip to Yakima, for Dad's doctor appointment the next morning, we'd buy tent material. Then we'd spend the afternoon making new money bags, cleaning the money, filling bags, and taking them to a coin shop.

Doctor Mead was a family friend who had long been aware of Dad's reduced capacities, closely monitoring his physical and mental health, and allowing him to continue driving. Dad glowed in the sun of Dr. Mead's respect and worked hard to appear normal for each office visit. The strain caused him to collapse in confusion the following day. Mom would prop him up until he was better.

Robin went to observe the appointment. Alice and I found a canvas maker. It was noon when we drove back home for lunch.

The coin laundry was set up in the family room. Dad laid a piece of 4x8 plywood across two sawbucks, and we set up stations around the makeshift table. My job was sewing canvas bags; Robin washed the grubby money in a soapy dishpan. Mom dried with an embroidered dish towel; Alice filled the new bags with shiny coins. The smell of detergent and silver hovered with Dad, as he wandered around ready to help. The whole process took a couple of hours.

My new acquaintance with junk silver led me to mistakenly think the face value needed to be counted. There was a reputable coin dealer in Seattle, with a coin-counting machine. They closed at 5 o'clock. As soon as the laundering was finished, with the bags of washed money loaded into the back of Robin's van, we dashed over the mountains to get there before closing. Dad stayed home. Seattle traffic was tough, and time was ticking. Minutes before 5 o'clock, the van's sagging rear end scraped the curb in front of the Second Avenue coin shop, and jerked to a stop. Curious street people watched us rush the heavy bags and coffee cans through the shop's door with a sigh of relief.

The open maw of the coin sorter swallowed the first of our silver and began noisily digesting. Suddenly it stopped. The money was still wet! It wouldn't work in the machine!

148 *River of Dementia*

Here we were on Second Avenue in downtown Seattle at quitting time, unable to count our moist money, and uneasy about leaving Dad alone overnight. The coin shop owner offered an empty room above the shop where the coins could be spread to dry overnight. With little choice, we left the money and drove back to Dad.

Early the next morning we called the coin shop. The balance left of $20,000, buried in the ground for twenty years, was... $12,113.55! Was it face value or weight? No one knew enough to ask. Dad lost a third of the money he originally paid. PT Barnum was right. "There's a sucker born every minute."

Happy ending? Mom invested the $12,000 in the 1995 magic of Microsoft stock. After several splits and a couple of years, it grew to over $80,000.

CHAPTER EIGHTEEN
Robert Ditches Pauline
1994—1995

Another old-fashioned Christmas at the farm. The lighted star hung over the front porch, with the sign, *Only Wise Men Seek Him*. Inside, on the mantle, under the Caucasian picture of Jesus, fourteen stockings hung, one for each family member, young and old. Mom loved the busy season and was the perfect elf to blend the sacred and secular, spreading the holiday spirit and a buffet of holiday treats, pies, and endless cookies. New Year's passed, and we began a mind-blowing 1995.

Focusing day by day on a failing husband, Mom mostly ignored the big picture. Church was a large part of their lives and had taken much of my parents' attention. As a child, I'd been jealous of the time they spent. They were devoted physically and financially, tithing regularly, serving as Sunday school teachers, board members, fundraising committee members. They participated in running Bible schools and confirmation classes, set up the manger scene at Christmas and served breakfast after Easter Sunrise

Service. Mom worked as church secretary, on and off, over the years. As a shy child, I felt lost.

When we moved over the mountains in 1958, the small Baptist Church in town received their focus and charity. For the next twenty years, Mom and Dad were entwined in Baptist Church leadership. Then, in 1994, Dad's relationship with the little church changed. Something was off. He was looking forward to becoming a deacon because of his long and generous service. Dad was denied, very unexpectedly, but Mom was accepted. Then, after two decades of setting up and taking down the Christmas Nativity scene, he was asked not to help and removed from the committee. Mom was mum. Later, we found out a lot of things Mom kept to herself.

That spring, after the valley farmers had burned the ditches to rid them of vegetation, ensuring free-flowing water, Mom looked out the kitchen window and saw Dad pushing a hand truck out the hedged driveway. Curious, she slipped out the back door and followed him. He turned down the road toward town. As Mom got closer, she could see that on his hand truck he'd put a car battery, two cans of motor oil, an electric lamp, and an alarm clock. Puzzled, she continued to catch up and called out "Robert, where are you going?"

He looked back at her and started to run, his hand truck bumping against the asphalt edge of the road. She hurried after him calling, "Robert! What are you doing!"

To her astonishment, he stopped, left his hand truck, and jumped into the irrigation ditch running beside the road. Mom was flabbergasted. When she got to him he looked at her sheepishly, like a little boy caught and in trouble.

An irrigation ditch is what it sounds like. It's used in farming communities to carry water to the fields. The ditches are about six feet wide and four feet deep, with steep sides that allow them to carry a maximum amount of water, moving alongside the roads throughout the valley. The ditch in front of our farm had about three feet of water, used to water the acreage, but also to keep the front lawn lush and green through the scorching summers. Each week, Mom or Dad would open a small gate and divert the water to flood the lawn and garden for an hour or two, then divert it back into the ever-flowing ditch.

Now, Dad, in water up to the thighs of his blue coveralls, tried, with chagrin, to crawl up the steep bank. Because there was no long grass to hold on to, he slipped and fell back into the water. Mom leaned down and tried to pull him out, but the height of the roadbed made the distance from Dad so far that she wasn't strong enough. She was beside herself, when a blue pickup truck came down the road, passed them slowly, and pulled over. Out stepped their good neighbor, Milo Sorensen, to ask if he could help. He was a big man and pulled Dad out easily. When Dad was out of the ditch, he told Milo that he had fallen in by accident and was thankful for the rescue. Dad was wily about hiding his follies. They laughed together, and Mom buttoned her lip. Another humiliation diverted. She'd been covering up a lot lately.

I realized later that in Dad's mind it made sense. He was running away. His shrewd, jumbled brain told him to take a battery for power, oil to keep the battery running, a lamp for light, and a clock to keep track of time.

Though his reason was faltering, his knack for acting had fooled everyone, even after digging up $20,000.00 in the ground. But the church was wary. A few good friends were wondering. Neighbors were watching. Mom was pretending he was okay out of deep love and faithfulness. His doctor helped her understand that Dad was ill, but he allowed him to drive and live a regular life. She prayed her help would be enough.

May 1995 was an exciting month for Morrie and me when our offer on a new home was accepted. Mom and Dad came for a visit to see it. Because it hadn't closed and the owners were still living there, we rented a boat to see it from the water. Morrie pulled the throttle to accelerate, and the prow of the boat reared up, attempting to come to a plane. Too much weight in the back. I tried lying on the covered bow for balance, and the boat leveled. As I lay keeping the bow down, Dad grabbed my foot, worried that Morrie was putting me in danger of falling off. I was secure; it wasn't going to happen. His overreaction was a sign of his growing fragility. The house was beautiful from the water, the boat ride pleasant, and Dad held onto my ankle the whole trip, a loving gesture, a wrinkle in the shrinking canvas of his sail.

After twenty-one years, we were trading a ten-acre farm for the waterfront; my attention was on moving. What I didn't know was that the pressure cooker at the farm was about to blow.

CHAPTER NINETEEN
Killing Kats
Spring 1995

"Bob! What have you done!" Pauline's voice held horror.

"I know," he said. "But what was I supposed to do? Wait until they overran the place?"

He went to get a shovel to dig a hole and bury them.

Snoqualmie (Sno-KWAL-mee), a Salish word for moon, is one of three main passes crossing Washington's Cascade mountain range between eastern and western Washington. An ancient Indian trail, used in the 1800s for cattle drives or mining supplies, it gained dependability in 1909 when the wagon road was improved along with the laying of railroad tracks. Starting in the winter of 1931-32 the pass was plowed all season and kept open as much as possible, year-round. It was finally paved in 1934.

A familiar old foe I've traveled all my life, I love its wild and ever-changing beauty. In summer the lakes sparkle, blue, giant fir trees line the roadside in crowded congregations touching the sky, and the mountain air is hot and pungent with woodsy spices. In winter, the landscape is covered in cathedral white lace or smothered in flakes of angel dust. The frozen air is clean and biting.

Today, the road is bare and wet, the sky overcast-grey, like my worry about Dad. He's been having trouble lately. "Something's happened with his church," I told Morrie. "even though he's been giving his all to the little Baptist Church since he stopped commuting."

"Maybe he's offended the church members? You know how stubborn he can be," Morrie said. "Remember last year when he kept needling you about looking at hot tubs in the middle of Mother's Day? You were really annoyed. No respect for your decision."

"You're right." I said, "his insistence made me angry. If he's been treating the church members that way, I can understand their concern. Then there are the trips into town where he's getting lost." I held my chin in thought. "Mom said he can't call home because he can't remember their number, and if he could, he can't dial the phone; she has to do it for him. His doctor still allows him to drive, but when do we take away his keys? And that goofy answering machine message she made him record. He sounds feeble. "Hello. This is Robert Davison, talking on the answering machine..." Mom shouldn't use it.

"She's just trying to make him feel important," Morrie said. "But you can tell something's gone wrong with him. His lists on cash register tape are a foot long! And his locks." Morrie shook his head. "He's got to lock up everything three times."

"The bananas and the whole buried money thing are so bizarre," I added. "Pop lived to almost 103, and Dad thinks he will, too. But Dad's going downhill. I wonder about Alzheimer's."

"Maybe you should look into it," Morrie said.

I could see new green leaves sprouting on the hedge as we turned into the farm's driveway. Unloading bags didn't take long, but walking toward the house I nearly stumbled over a small, grey kitten that wobbled under my feet. The aroma of chocolate, nuts, and butter welcomed me at the back door. My mouth watered.

"What's wrong with the grey kitten?" I asked, dropping my bags on the bright-patterned kitchen floor, "It's acting odd."

Mom lifted the last chocolate chip cookie from the pan and gave me a big hug. "Well," she rinsed her hands, and sighed, "I can't imagine what your dad was thinking."

She paused, considering what she wanted to say. I waited. I could tell by her indecision that she wanted to protect him, but this time there was no defense, no excuse.

"While I was doing the bulletin at church last week, he put the latest litter of barn kittens and their mom in a cardboard box, closed the lid, and tried to gas them." She looked down, twisting the wedding ring on her finger. "Something went wrong and not all of them died." My eyes squeezed tight trying to blot out the image. "The grey is one of three left, but they're not quite right. He told me he thought it would be more humane to gas them than to stuff them in a gunny sack with a brick and throw them into the river." I cringed, recalling the old-fashioned practice. "I told him I would have taken them to the pound."

"That's horrible!" Goosebumps prickled my arms. "What's the matter with him? The pound would have given them a chance. These kittens are damaged. Doesn't he understand the cruelty?"

"I don't know." Her voice was pained. She took off her apron and hung it in the pantry. "He was unhappy when it failed, but now he's just ignoring what happened."

Dad was distant when I asked about the kittens later. He didn't say much, only that he'd botched the job and was sorry. Then he grabbed his red plaid, flannel work jacket and disappeared outside, as the back door slammed. His lack of judgment was alarming. I had only known him as reliable, kind, and gentle; he'd always stood for thoughtfulness and honesty. He tried to live the Ten Commandments. Killing kittens didn't fit. I looked out over the green fields trying to find a reason for his terrible judgment.

The farm is a garden of Eden in the spring, filled with daffodils and lilacs, blossoming fruit trees humming with bees, birds twittering in the orchard and surrounding poplars. There was no place for Dad's strange brutality.

On my list of farm favorites: the big swing; the fresh, buttered, corn from the nearby field; the skating rink in the winter; but first place goes to the sleeping porch at the top of the farmhouse stairs. Open the door, and you're outside, in a small eyrie, surrounded by screen. Two sleeping platforms on either side are covered by comfy mattresses ready for sleeping bags. Warm weather or cold, it is the best place to sleep, ever. Facing east, you can look across the front porch roof, down onto the road or front lawn, and watch the comings and goings. In the afternoon of a hot day, shade comes early, and keeping your head low, no one need know you are up there reading a book or taking a nap.

For me, the best time on the sleeping porch is during a thunderstorm, with lightning streaking in the distance, rain pounding the roof, breathing the fresh essence of wet earth and hay, cozy in a sleeping bag tucked up to my chin. Mom and Dad keep the porch clean and ready, so sleeping there is always a treat.

In the morning, as I helped load breakfast dishes in the dishwasher, Mom said, "Dad's wandering at night. Sometimes I wake up and find his side of the bed empty, so I search the barn, the shop, the garage, everywhere, until I find him. He's always happy to see me and says he couldn't find his way back. He's beginning to wander almost every night. Last week I found him in the barn. He said he couldn't find the door and was very glad to see me." She noticed my troubled look. "Don't worry, he's fine during the day." She smiled in resignation. "He putters with his projects, but I don't think I dare leave him alone again." Her eyes looked weary, but Mom was never a quitter.

"We'll come anytime you need us," I said.

"I know." She closed the dishwasher and went upstairs.

Later, as we were leaving, I hugged her and Dad, then slid into the Subaru beside Morrie. "Let us know if you need us," I reminded them.

Time only aggravated the situation.

Dad's night-wandering continued, and a new distrustful nature appeared. "Mom locked me in the barn one night," he told me. "She sat there on a hay bale watching and laughing, while I looked for the door. She didn't let me out until she was ready." Same picture, different lens.

He mocked the way she looked. "You can see right through her hair," he'd smirk, referring to the pink scalp under her pixie haircut. His devotion became suspicion and contempt. In his mind, Mom was stealing his money. He hid "evidence" under the cargo floor of his Suburban and whispered the secret to my sister Robin. When she unscrewed the floorboard, there was nothing but a few meaningless papers and receipts.

Mom and Dad had been together more than fifty-six years as companions, best friends, lovers, and playmates; they'd been lampooned as the "Bobbsey Twins" because of their tight bond. Now, at 77, my sweet, cheerful, gutsy mom was facing swirling eddies on an uncharted river, as the man she married more than a half-century ago, was drifting away. Memory loss, confusion, suspicion, night wandering, ridicule, and now killing kittens. Water was sloshing in the bottom of his boat, and the hole was getting larger. Mom thought his skiff was named Senility. She was saving her distress signal.

My sisters were upset about Dad's recent behavior and Alice suggested that Mom should have Dad's power of attorney in the future. Luckily, Dad was "on" the day they saw their lawyer in Yakima, and he signed the paperwork without hesitation. This was important later when he ran into trouble with the sheriff.

CHAPTER TWENTY
Measuring the Bathroom
June 1995

He stepped across the bathroom threshold and wondered why he was here. Nature wasn't calling so it must be something else. Maybe it was to measure something. Yes, measuring. That was it. But how could he measure without a ruler or measuring tape? He thought a minute and then had an idea. He stripped off all his clothing and held his undershorts, stretching the waistband. Yes, this might work. He stooped down and started carefully calculating. One, two, three waistbands to the wall. One, two....

The exhaust from the blue Chevy Suburban had been spewing into the cold air for ten minutes. Mom, Alice, Robin, and their children waited for Dad to come out of the house to go to Yakima. He said he'd only be a minute.

"I wonder what's keeping him?" Alice shifted to a more comfortable position.

"Oh, Bob!" Mom harrumphed as she got out of the front seat. "I'll go get him." She huffed toward the back door.

"Bob, are you coming?" she called out through the downstairs rooms. No answer. She went up the stairs and checked the bedrooms. Not there. She opened the bathroom door at the end of the hallway... and froze. "Bob! What are you doing?" Her hand flew to cover her mouth. Dad was naked, holding his briefs. He'd been using them as a ruler while he stooped, to measure the bathroom floor. His eyes were childlike, a deer caught in the headlights. She stood speechless with shock. Mom was not prepared. She had encountered many unusual moments with Dad lately but seeing him rashly exposed threw her. She led him to their bedroom and told him to get dressed. Knocked off balance, she returned to the Suburban, and with confused disgust blurted, "He was naked. Measuring the bathroom. With his underwear!" She might have spared the grandchildren had she not been panicked. Her shame and anger were masking the fear she felt. They made the trip to Yakima, but the fat was in the fire.

For thirty-five years Dad had run his own floor covering business, measuring the dimensions of rooms for carpet, linoleum, tile or vinyl, estimating costs for potential customers. He had built the needed bathroom addition when they moved to the farm in 1958, and in his befuddled mind, what he was doing probably made sense. Dad was funny and quirky as we grew up. We were accustomed to his unique way of life, but when we heard the story, it was a smack in the head for all of us.

I sent for a packet of information from the Alzheimer's Association. Did he have Alzheimer's? When the packet came, there were helpful details about the disease, one of many under the umbrella of dementia-like progression, stages of decline, what to expect at each level and the final days when the patient stops eating because swallowing becomes impossible. His early symptoms mimicked Alzheimer's but were not quite the same. Mom would have provided much better care with foresight from the Alzheimer's Association, but she wouldn't read the material. She was afraid he'd catch her and be angry. She preferred being blind. Admitting his mind was broken was betrayal. Mom was loyal to a fault, had a servant's heart, and honored her husband's infallibility. She was able to accept things as normal that weren't and go along cheerfully taking care of him as she always had.

Without experience, it was hard to understand what was happening. Dad's puzzle pieces were slow to come together. Robin held an odd-shaped piece when her third baby was born in November of 1993. Mom came to help during granddaughter Emily's first week—Mom and Dad helped with all the new grandbabies—but this time Dad stayed home. Then he pestered Mom, over the phone, to come back to the farm. He kept complaining about how cold he was at night. Mom always ran hot, and during the winter kept the house furnace down as she worked her busy day and very low at night to save money. When I lived at home, my electric blanket was a blessed winter necessity. Why didn't he turn up the furnace for his needs? Was his metabolism changing with his disease? Dad was adrift without Mom. She went home early to find him sleeping on a cot, in a sleeping bag, in the bathroom where it was warm. To be in competition with his new granddaughter was strange.

"*Happy Birthday dear Robin,*" we sang in unison, "*Happy Birthday to you.*" It was four-month-old baby

Emily's first visit to the farm. She came to celebrate her mama's thirty-ninth birthday and slept in Grandma Pauline and Grandpa Robert's bedroom to give her parents a full night's sleep.

The next morning, Dad pulled Robin aside. "Your Mom is doing things with my money," he whispered. "I want you to take this cash and keep it for me." He handed her one hundred, one-dollar bills.

"Are you sure?" Robin looked at him quizzically. "That seems odd, Dad." He bobbed his head in silent affirmation and walked off.

As Morrie had reminded me earlier, Dad's behavior last year had been irksome. Fifteen or so family members had come to our home to celebrate Mother's Day with Mom. I was juggling meal-serving, visiting, and cleanup, when Dad playfully invited me to come see a large hot tub he and Mom were buying from a store not far from our house. I was too busy and said no thanks. My sisters, aunts, uncles, and cousins had driven more than an hour to get to Gig Harbor and I wanted to visit with them. Dad would not take "no" for an answer. He cajoled. He wheedled. He badgered me, just short of begging. At 45, with five children, I felt minimized, disrespected, and disgusted. I gave in with resentment.

In hindsight, I realize why he was fixated on the hot tub. He no longer felt safe taking the trailer and the family to California. The hot tub meant vacationing at home without admitting he was weakening. He had the farmhouse enlarged with two new rooms and filled one room with the 8x12 foot tub. He planned to use the tub as a swimming pool and not a spa, so he kept the temperature at 80°. If Mom or Dad ever used it, I wasn't around. He did so many nice things in his life, blending love and anxiety.

This compulsion happened again one weekend when we arrived at the farm to find Dad excited to show us a new, compact Chinook motorhome. We joined his excitement and drove to see the beautiful, small "home on wheels" in Yakima. Until then, we didn't know Dad needed Mom's assistance in the bathroom when away from home. Since he loved to go somewhere each day, he'd have to use the women's restroom. Traveling with a lavatory would solve his dilemma; he didn't realize they couldn't afford it. Still good at clever solutions, he was out of touch with reality.

Dad's measuring of the bathroom should have been enough, but we were ignorant. Nothing like this had ever happened in our family memory. Strange currents were carrying him farther and farther away. Dad was becoming unrecognizable. Each time he tumbled over a waterfall, it took him longer to resurface and catch his breath.

CHAPTER TWENTY-ONE
Class Reunion
July 1995

I felt like Alice in Wonderland. Our world was getting "curiouser and curiouser" as Dad slipped down the rabbit hole.

Mid-morning, in mid-July we pulled into the farm driveway to find Dad in the front yard, carrying an opened can of tuna fish which he set on the home-made barbecue. He'd constructed the very large barbecue years earlier. In the fifties he ran across a round, red Coca-Cola sign, at least four feet in diameter. Today, it would be a valuable antique. The convex side was covered with porcelain, for the shiny logo, the concave side made of steel. He turned the sign upside down, like a bowl, attached four galvanized pipe legs to its red underside, and it made a great fire pit. For years, the barbecue perched on the green lawn of the farmhouse like an empty-headed alien; countless hotdog and marshmallow roasts partied there.

Dad was inventive. Clever carpentry projects and solutions, like making me a car swing, kept his bright mind occupied. He also believed in the power of words. He and Mom loved learning big words: sagacity, corpulence, or precursor.

His reading was not wide, but deep. The Bible, his first choice; books about religion; books and magazines about travel, agriculture, and health—he was an advocate of nutritionist Adelle Davis and valued natural foods. His favorite reading material, though, was the monthly *Reader's Digest*, a diverse collection of traditional information. To encourage us to read, he gave all of us annual *Reader's Digest* gift subscriptions. Mom kept them coming for years after he was gone.

Dad's conservative values and high school education kept him grounded. Though he moved near a college town and helped us girls with a college degree, he didn't trust higher education. For him, flying too high was frightening.

Mom read lovely stories to us when we were little. Fairy tales, Raggedy Ann and Andy, Doctor Dolittle, and Uncle Wiggily live fondly in my memory. My love of reading comes from Mom. She read every night before sleeping and kept a large library of favorite books for us to read: *A Girl of the Limberlost, Ruth Fielding of the Red Mill, Alice in Wonderland, The Wizard of Oz, The Mill and the Floss*. In later years she treasured her expurgated *Reader's Digest Condensed Books* and didn't mind losing some of each story, so she could read more.

We had traveled to the farm that day for my high school reunion in the evening. Out of the car, the blazing heat hugged our bodies.

"What's the can of tuna fish for?" I asked Dad.

"I'm killing the ground hornets," he said. "I mixed rat poison with the tuna and now I'll leave it out for the hornets to find. They'll take the poisoned fish back to their larva where it will kill the whole hive." He set the open can on the barbecue.

"Aren't you going to cover it so kids and cats won't get poisoned?"

"Leave it alone. Nothing's going to happen." He walked across the green grass peevishly. After the cat gassing and bathroom measuring, I was worried.

Inside, the house was cool, and Mom was pouring whirred raspberries onto waxed paper to make fruit leather, a healthy treat for the grandkids. Her love language being pie, spread across the counter were apple, chocolate, and bumbleberry.

"What's up with Dad? He's grouchy."

"I know. He's been more cantankerous lately, probably because he doesn't sleep much at night." She rinsed her hands and untied her apron. "I never know what to expect," she sighed. "Most of the time he's the sweet man I married, then suddenly I'm with an irritated stranger."

"He's different now," I agreed and hoisted my suitcase upstairs.

I unpacked, hung up my party dress, and laid out my evening accessories, eager to see my high school buddies at the reunion.

After lunch, I found an empty cardboard milk carton in the kitchen, cut a small hole in one side, and cut the bottom off. Then I took it outside and placed it over the can of poisoned tuna. Now Dad's hornet trap was safe from cats and children.

Winnapaw High School, a small, country school, was holding a multi-class reunion. Although my sister Alice and I are two grades apart, we'd celebrate together. She and her family arrived later in the afternoon and we headed upstairs to get ready. The dinner at the Elks Club started at six o'clock. A warm evening breeze rustled the leaves of the elm trees and ruffled our dresses as we walked to the car. The summer sun was not yet down, though crickets had begun their ticking. Dad, following us, spied my make-do cover over the tuna can. He charged toward the barbecue and swatted the carton to the ground.

"Hey! That was to keep the cats out." I was irked.

"I told you to leave it alone." He stomped the milk carton under his foot, picked it up and walked away.

I caught Alice's rolling eyes. Again, this behavior was not our easy-going Dad. Though we laughed it off, apprehension squeezed tighter.

The evening hours flew as we mined the last forty years. I had found wonderful and genuine friends during my two-and-a-half years at Winnapa High School. Raucous laughter played along with music and shared memories, long lost.

At Edmonds High School, I had been a small fish in my class of almost two hundred. Moving to Winnapa in my sophomore year, I became a big fish in my school class of twenty-four. Visiting with decades-old classmates was a romp of reminiscence.

We came home late and slept on the sleeping porch, a perfect place to stay as the house cooled down. It was a warm, no-covers, night. In spite of the pleasure of the evening, a sense of unease hovered as I fell asleep. I dreamed I was crawling above a rushing river on a broken wooden bridge, with many of the planks missing.

CHAPTER TWENTY-TWO
No Picnic
July 1995

Sunday morning after the reunion, I woke up on the sleeping porch in the silken air of another spectacular summer day. Cornfields glimmered in the sunshine. Horses in the neighboring pastures stood twitching in the warmth of the early morning sun. The breath of breeze drying the dewy grass gave no whisper of the storm ahead.

Mom's homemade cinnamon rolls were delicious for breakfast before church, and as we ate, we laughed together, revisiting last night's party. Dad asked about the reunion picnic that afternoon and wondered when it started. Since picnics had always been one of his favorite pleasures, I was afraid he wanted to go and worried that after his latest missteps, he might humiliate himself.

"We've decided not to go," I said, catching Alice's questioning blue eyes in the dining room mirror.

"Oh, you don't want to miss it," he said smiling. "It will be fun to see everyone and it's such a nice day."

I changed direction. "We'd rather go for a ride to the U-

Tote-Em and get ice cream." I thought I had him. He loved the U-Tote-Em's "King Kong Kones," as he jokingly called them. "I'd rather go to the picnic," he said, putting down his Bible.

"No, no, no," I laughed, "we'd rather have ice cream!" I had no idea what would happen by skipping the picnic.

After church, we piled into the old blue Suburban. Morrie drove, Dad rode in the co-pilot seat. I sat behind Dad, Alice sat behind Morrie, and Mom sat happily in the middle between her girls. The afternoon was hot enough to see heat waves shimmer from the blacktop, intensifying the scent of fresh-cut hay floating over the valley. Even on Sundays the mowers and rakes were working to get the second cutting of hay dried and in the barn.

The U-Tote-Em was favored by college students and townspeople, with juicy hamburgers and giant soft-serve cones. Alice had worked there as a teen. The drive-thru was empty. Morrie drove in the wrong way so I could order from the passenger side. This seemed to bother Dad, who was sitting in front of me. He was embarrassed about coming in the wrong direction, not following the rules. He rolled down his window to courteously greet the waitress and apologize. We were both in front of her, but as I began to ask for two large, soft-serve chocolate cones and three large half-and-half cones, the girl was focusing on me and ignored Dad's polite greeting. When she returned with the first cones, he spoke to her again, with no acknowledgment. Reading her actions as rude and dismissive, when the girl brought the remaining cone, he began shouting out of his open window, *"I'm Robert Davison, goddammit, and I've lived in this damn valley for thirty-seven goddamn years and you bastards have no right to treat me..."*

The shock of Dad's outburst was like smacking into a clear glass door that looked open. I suddenly found myself ducked down in mortification thinking, "I've got to sit up! I've got to sit up!" I did, grabbing the last cone. Morrie hit the gas pedal and Alice circled her finger around her ear, the crazy sign, for the startled girl. Mom was flabbergasted.

Hot air blasted in Dad's open window as he shook his fist and continued yelling, *"You bastards, my name is Robert Davison and I've lived in this goddamned valley for thirty-seven years..."* on and on, as Morrie raced through streets and alleys, past the empty rodeo grounds, then the Bi-Mart, to get out of town and hearing distance! We were stunned! We'd never heard him curse. He was virtuous, soft-spoken, and dignified. He'd spent his life being respectable, a principled example for others, a sweet and gentle father. His behavior was demented. Who was this crazy person?

As Morrie roamed the countryside, our ice cream melted from the heat streaming through Dad's open window. We licked the dribbles on autopilot. Silence. Only our eyes spoke. I looked at Alice in wonder. Her eyes answered in nervous bemusement. Mom stared in wide-eyed helplessness. Our normal nervous laughter vanished. We were afraid speech might bring on another tirade. This was new territory. What was safe to say to our frenzied dad? I peered out the window, not seeing the tedding machines turning over the rows of hay to dry. My mind kept rerunning the scene at the drive-In.

Dad's rage began to morph into cheerfulness. He loved taking rides with family and friends. The hot breeze through his window, and the open road soothed him.

"When is a quah not a quah?" he chuckled. "When it's Stillaguamish." His laughter was merry. The old joke was his attempt to distract us from the unmentionable. Mom shook her head, fingers covering her mouth. We were anxious to get him home. Morrie turned left to head for the farm and as the heavy Suburban slowed for the turn, Dad opened his door, stepped to the running board, and jumped to the ground. Morrie slammed on the brakes.

"Dad! Get back in the car." Alice laughed, attempting lightheartedness.

"Not if we're going home," he grinned playfully, sweat gleaming on his forehead.

Morrie nodded. "Okay, we can drive around a little more."

We drove for another ten minutes and then turned left on our way home. Dad jumped down again! Each time we turned toward the farm, Dad jumped down, beaming like a naughty schoolboy. We kept calm and humored him, not wanting him to explode again.

Finally, in desperation, Morrie stopped the Suburban, leaned on top of his 83-year-old father-in-law, holding him down, while Alice rushed from behind, into the driver's seat, and dashed for home like a Ferrari for the checkered flag. The day was bizarre and baffling, but not over.

Alice parked the Suburban in the shade of a barnyard tree and everyone hurried to the back door with relief. The house was a cocoon of cool for our inflamed emotions. Everyone went inside except Dad. He stood in the sizzling sun, beside our parked Subaru, and lifted the wipers away from the windshield to point outward. It was 98° in the shade. No one could entice him into the house. We learned later that by pointing the windshield wipers out, he was secretly signaling he wanted to come home with us. He didn't want to stay with Mom.

Alice and Mom, afraid of triggering Dad, paced in the house, watching him out the window. Morrie and I, willing to try persuasion, went out to join him. He stood there, quietly, unfazed by the perturbing heat.

"I want to go to your house," he said.

"You can't go home with us, Dad." The memory crushes my heart. Deserting him felt awful, but he was too troubled to leave the farm. "You have things to do here, and Mom needs you." Lame. Reason meant little to his agitated brain. "You need to take care of Mom."

"It's hot as hell out here," Morrie tried. "Let's go in and get something cool to drink." Dad just stood there stubbornly, adrenaline stoking his resolve. After a while, Morrie walked away to get Dad some lemonade.

Logic, persuasion, begging made no difference. After a long while, we gathered in the house to strategize. Alice found the number of a county social worker in the phone book and called. He arrived, tried his best, but couldn't move Dad. The social worker told us the next step was to call the sheriff. That was hard. Heatstroke might have been better than what happened next.

Dust rose as a sheriff's cruiser pulled into the driveway and stopped in front of Dad, who was standing next to us. Mom and Alice peeked from the kitchen. Two sheriff's deputies got out. "Hello, Mr. Davison, do you know why we're here?"

"Hello, officers," Dad said jovially as if this were a

social visit.

"Your family is worried and wants you to go into the house. Will you do this?"

Dad shook his head no.

They talked to him, with kindness and respect, for forty-five minutes, while Morrie and I listened. Finally, they explained that they would have to take him to jail if he wouldn't return to the house. He refused to cooperate. With a profound sense of disbelief, I watched the two officers push my dear Dad onto the hood of their cruiser and cuff his hands behind his back. The deputies walked Dad to the rear door and when he wouldn't get in, placed him on his stomach on the plastic-covered back seat. As they were leaving, I opened his door to reassure him. "We'll meet you there, Dad. We'll be right behind you!"

"You've never done what I wanted," he spat.

Though I chuckled at the irony, a barbed vine slashed my heart.

CHAPTER TWENTY-THREE
Psych 101
July 1995

Uff da! This day was unbelievable! An imp emerged in our midst, his mischief led him to the Ellensburg Jail, and from there, to Yakima Valley Memorial Hospital. Mom, Alice, and I followed Dad. Morrie drove to the coast for work the next day.

The elevator stopped on the psychiatric floor and opened in front of massive, grey doors. Intimidating. A sign by the wall phone directed us to call for permission to enter. We called, were questioned, and the heavy metal doors parted slowly as if entering Ali Baba's cave. Instead of golden treasure, a large high-ceilinged lounge lay before us, a murmur of conversation, and patients wearing street clothes, reading, talking quietly, or walking around. No lunatic asylum like my Grandma Alice had been in. Large, dark windows ran across one side of the fifth-floor area, promising a lush view of the Yakima Valley harvest when the sun rose. We checked in at the nurses' station and went to find Dad. He had been assigned a small, tidy, single room.

"Hi, Dad. Are you all set here?" We waited to assess his mood.

"Yes," he said, then whispered, "they are reading my thoughts with an instrument. They put it in my ear to listen." I knew it must be a digital thermometer but didn't want to argue.

"Where is Morrie?" he asked.

"He had to go back home to teach tomorrow."

"When do you have to go back home?" He wondered.

"I'm not sure," I said. "I might stay awhile."

We sat with him and chatted about simple things, nothing that would upset him, while he took in the unfamiliar surroundings.

What complete fools, he thought. I should never have been brought here. I just needed to get away from the farm and Pauline. "Eat your chicken! Eat your chicken!" she says. Always nagging about something. Why couldn't we go to the picnic? Dumb clucks couldn't even help me get away. I'll pretend to go along here so I can get out, but they can hear my thoughts, so I'd better think about Bible verses when the doctors come. Those damn sheriff's deputies should have stayed out of it. I just want to go home. Even Pauline would be better than this.

It was difficult when it was time to leave him; however, we were all exhausted. This was the strangest day of my life. Unimaginable before, and now the beginning of a new reality.

Robin arrived Monday and we hurried back to the hospital. Thankfully, there had been no problems and he greeted us happily when we entered his room. He'd had breakfast, was dressed and shaved, and ready to go home. The fangs of disloyalty bit hard as I had to tell him he couldn't leave. Why was I always the delegated spokesperson? I am the oldest daughter, but also, Alice found Dad's situation hard to face, Mom was befuddled, and Robin generously followed my lead.

The doctors planned to find appropriate medication and dosage during his stay. Available drugs like memantine, tacrine, or galantamine would be tried to control his psychosis. If successful, he might be home by Friday.

Dad was on his best behavior throughout the week, determined to convince the doctors that holding him was a mistake. He was a master actor and had long been using his talent to fool family, friends, doctors, neighbors, anyone who needed convincing he was fine. This had worked until now.

Dad's time in the psych ward was draining for us. We'd awake in disbelief, drive to Yakima, spend the day with Dad, and drive back home in the dark. When we weren't at the hospital, we'd go over and over Dad's state of affairs, a jumble with an unpredictable future. There was nothing to do but float with him on his frightening trip.

With ups and downs, he shortly began to improve as the medicine took effect. Alice and Robin went home on Wednesday and by the end of the week, Dad was back to reality, his medications effective. Friday afternoon we packed him up and took him home, in high spirits, happy to be free.

Mom was grateful to have him home again, and fixed chicken and dumplings, his favorite dinner; food was always an important part of his day. As we spoke cautiously with Dad, Mom and I conversed with our eyes as we had in the hospital. It was a happy evening, Mom and I staying focused on Dad's behavior. At bedtime, he climbed the stairs to their bedroom, gladly. Sleeping in his own bed that night would be a luxury.

With Dad home and in bed, we breathed a sigh of relief, cleaned the kitchen, and put his hospital clothes in the wash. Mom was emptying things from his white, plastic hospital bag when she paled and said, "I forgot to pick up his medicine!" I'd thought we'd brought his meds from the hospital. This was bad. The stores in Ellensburg closed at 6:00 p.m. and wouldn't open until morning.

I woke at dawn, determined to get Dad's medications ASAP. As I pulled on my shorts and threw on my tank top, I thought about my parents' marriage. Mom, like a flame, full of potential to conquer the world, and Dad, a gentle breeze trying to control that flame. They combined two very different elements to keep life warm for us as we grew up. Now the air for Mom's flame is sputtering. She could deal with it. She's handled a loveless childhood and two lost babies, raised four children while Dad commuted, lost Carol to cancer, and worked through Dad's stroke and heart trouble. She took exceptional care of Pop and she would take exceptional care of Pop's child, for that is what Dad was becoming. She would carry the heavy end of their love story.

I followed the aroma of coffee down the stairs to the kitchen where Dad was pouring berry syrup over his waffle.

"We have to run to the pharmacy." I poured myself a cup of ebony energy.

"The social worker is coming to talk about options at nine," Mom said. "There's not enough time to make it to town and back."

This was frustrating but I couldn't go myself and leave Mom alone. In hindsight, we should have put the meeting off and rushed to the pharmacy.

While we waited, Mom chopped walnuts for brownies, and I lingered over my coffee. Dad finished his breakfast and hovered. He paced the kitchen, uneasy about Mom's meeting. I'm sure he wanted to take charge. I meant to see he didn't.

"Want to go for a walk?" I asked him.

"No," he said tersely, watching out the kitchen windows.

At 9:00 a.m. a man drove into the lane and got out of his car. He was tall and slender, but, oddly, wearing a floppy black hat like a Kentucky moonshiner. What was he thinking?! I could feel Dad's hackles rising as he took in the man's appearance. A villain's black hat. Dad knew it! Mom was in danger! His paranoia took over.

The bottom level of the farmhouse is laid out in a circle from the back door, through the kitchen, through the den, rounding through the family room, the hot tub room, and back to the kitchen.

Mom met the social worker at the back door, led him through the kitchen to the den and closed the door, then closed the other door to the family room. I hustled Dad into the adjoining hot tub room, reminding him, "This is Mom's meeting. It's not polite to butt in." But Dad was electrified with fear.

He moved past the hot tub and stood near the open

door to the family room, listening intently. I was afraid he'd bolt so I stood in the doorway blocking his exit. We waited there, his shoulders tight in hypervigilance, his ears focused on the murmur of conversation coming from the den. Suddenly, he darted toward the door. I snatched a broom standing nearby and held it as a barrier in front of me, barring him from passing through. He grabbed the other side of the broom and we began the "broom dance," each pushing to gain territory.

"*No, Dad*! This is Mom's business." I pushed and he stepped back. "*No, Dad!*" He pushed forward in silence, concentrating on getting to Mom. "*It's okay*! Mom will only be a little while."

All of a sudden, he let go of the broom, slipped by me, shot through the family room, and burst into Mom's meeting. "Get out!" he shouted, his finger pointed at the man. "Get out of here! *Leave!*"

In the face of Dad's belligerence, the social worker got up quietly and walked through the kitchen toward the back door. Mom followed him, apologizing. Dad followed her. More melodrama. Part of our journey, as Dad was again sucked into the quicksand of rage. Chagrined, Mom and the social worker walked through the windowed back porch and into the yard. I followed behind Dad as he passed through the shady, yellow kitchen, his hand brushing the countertop then picking up the butcher knife Mom had left after cutting walnuts. He carried it toward the door. I froze. Not far behind him, life went into slow motion as he reached the porch, raised the butcher knife above his head and hurled it at the unsuspecting man. The sharp knife flew through the air forever, while I held my breath, envisioning the bloodied social worker with a butcher knife in his back. Finally, the big knife fell short. Thank goodness, Dad had lost his dexterity.

The frightened man skittered to his car and left. Mom stood dumbstruck, while Dad puffed on the porch triumphantly.

Here was a doppelgänger, a stranger. He looked like Dad, but only on the outside. Soon after, we began to refer to this imposter as John—the alias Pop gave him on his birth certificate—John Gilbert Davison. A fiction. Nothing like our gentle, caring, and faith-filled father.

Dumbfounded, Mom picked up the butcher knife and followed Dad back into the house unaware the social worker, fearing for our lives, had called the sheriff.

CHAPTER TWENTY-FOUR
Psych 102
August 1995

With a loud crunch of gravel, the sheriff's deputies spun into the driveway, worried that Dad might harm us. As they approached the screened back door, Dad met them on the stoop, his actor's face flushed.

"Hello gentlemen," he greeted them with a playful smile. Mom and I stood behind him, crowded in the doorway.

"Do you know why we're here, Mr. Davison?" Again, they were respectful and kind, but alert. "Yes I do, officers," he responded, grinning.

"We have to take you into custody. Will you come with us?" they asked politely.

"Nope," he said, shaking his head, his eyes beaming with mischief.

"I'll go with you, Dad," I said, trying to avoid another standoff.

"I'm sorry, Ma'am, but no one else is allowed to ride in

the patrol car."

"I'll go with you if she can come," John/Dad tried to best them with a sly bargain. I hoped this would save him from another dust up. Thank heavens, the deputies agreed.

I ducked into the back seat of the patrol car, my first time, unaware of what bodily fluids may have been there before me. A black mesh cage separated us from the deputies. As we drove out of the driveway, John/Dad leaned over to whisper in my ear, "I wish I could've hit him with a baseball bat!" My brain sizzled trying to absorb what was happening. Honest, soft spoken Dad was gone. I loved this person beside me and would do whatever it took to help him. But I was scared for Mom, for our family, and for myself. Where would we go from here?

Back to the Yakima hospital again. Mom and I made the same trip as before. Dad's trip had a detour. The seriousness of his knife-throwing charge meant he had to go before the court and be placed under a judge's jurisdiction.

When we entered his private room later, Dad wasn't there, only a shell holding his fear. His bravado was gone. We sat with him until the evening meal, then headed for the cafeteria. After an institutional dinner and another agonizing day, we dragged home.

During the following week, his broken brain cracked open and drained away any awareness he had left. Again, he believed his thoughts were being read with an instrument and was deeply afraid.

The second day, we met him in his room with hushed instructions, "Turn your chair with your back to the door and don't talk. Just write what you have to say on this paper. They're reading our lips and listening to our thoughts." We wrote notes to each other, with stub pencils he'd found, until he was called away. Our dark drama in the psych ward was an extreme contrast to the bright, sunny day outside. It was like being in a parallel universe. Everything was familiar, but horribly skewed. Dad had disappeared.

His controlling nature had always frustrated me, but that control made him feel safe. Being in charge of his world meant he could keep bad things from happening, and his anxious psyche could imagine many bad things. Slowly losing his control must be terrifying. Darkness, becoming a whirl of bewilderment, betrayal, and enemies. Trapped and afraid. No one to trust. Hell.

Later in the week our adult son Chris came to visit his grandpa. We sat on the psych ward's shaded veranda in a silky warm breeze. Dad bent close to his grandson and said in an undertone, "See the ivy over there?" He gestured toward a rosy brick wall covered with emerald ivy leaves and tendrils. "It has cameras and speakers in it so they can watch us and hear what we say. Turn away from it when you talk." Chris, for Grandpa's sake, played along.

Remembering this is like water torture. Each little drip of memory sends shards of pain. His torment was our torment. We absorbed his nightmare of panic and disorientation, without the ability to help him. I know now small, silent strokes in the brain cause brain tissue to die. With Dad the issue was in the area that controls paranoia. In his case the controls blew out, and his paranoia raced unchecked.

Surrounding Mom with love and support was the best

care we knew how to give. Alice, Robin and I drove her over the barren hills to Yakima each morning, spent the day together, and drove her home each night in the purple van. Dad insisted she buy it when he understood what was happening to himself, before we did. The van delighted her, as did his desire that she have it. Mom's favorite color was purple, the color of nobility, dignity and devotion. She faced Dad's disappearance with these qualities as well as deep faith and a hopeful spirit. She'd learned early in life to work hard and overlook the past, so this is how she would handle Dad's transmogrification. On their journey and after, the van stood as a touchstone of his love for her.

For several weeks the doctors studied him and tuned his medications. We knew he was getting better when he began trying to trick the doctors again. They weren't fooled. Finally, stabilized with new medicines, he was sent before a judge who remanded him to a nursing home in Ellensburg. John/Dad was now a ward of the court. He could make no move without the judge's permission.

The psychiatric floor in the Yakima hospital was spacious, light and airy. Dad had a private room. The custodial nursing home was clean but dreary, with brown and yellow decor from the seventies and the smell of Pine-sol. The facility was about a five on a scale of one to ten. Dad was locked into the Alzheimer's wing. The first night, he told Mom, a woman crawled into bed with him. It happened again the next few nights. Whether his nightmare was real or delusional, he was transferred to a double room in the regular wing where his friends brought his green recliner to make him more comfortable. His roommate looked comatose. We never met him or saw him move. He was always asleep, under his white sheet, when we visited. But John/Dad told us that the man "had prostitutes in at night and had sex with them in the bathroom." No genteel Dad here, only John.

Mom visited daily, and church friends and neighbors stopped by. John/Dad kept up a good face, though he must have been embarrassed. Bored with this dull routine the weeks crawled by with little hope of change.

"Look," I said to Morrie in late August. "Here's an article about a study at the University of Washington, testing people for Alzheimer's. I think this might work for Dad." I called Mom for approval and then the University. We were grateful when he was accepted for testing. The downside was waiting from July until mid-October for his first appointment.

In the meantime, Robin found an upgraded Alzheimer's facility in North Seattle and with the judge's permission, we moved Dad there to wait for his upcoming interview. It was a lovely place, blue and white, bright and pleasant, with safe outdoor paths for walking in the fresh air. Robin decorated his private room with familiar items, family photos, and furniture. A much-improved situation. As the weeks went by, he was visited by Seattle friends and relatives who couldn't see why he was in an Alzheimer's facility, given how normal he seemed. He was still a talented performer.

Mom was 77 years old, still vibrant, comfortable in her husband's direction, when he abruptly disappeared. Left with a ghost in a body, the heavy responsibility was hers to make future plans from the rubble of a broken life.

Dad was on target when he dug up the oily money last

spring. The farm would have to be sold. Mom loved her country paradise, but without Dad, there was no way she could keep it up by herself. And how else would she pay for his care? At over $4500 a month at the Seattle Alzheimer's facility, she could only afford a few months. The farm was their savings account. She would sell it and when that money was gone, they'd have to go on welfare. The large and abundant life they'd lived in the Badger Pocket would now become a fairytale in trade for Dad's care.

CHAPTER TWENTY-FIVE
Gone with the Windover
October 1995

Dry leaves scuttled and swirled on the windy, September weekend when friends and family gathered to load Mom's bed and dresser; the heavy Formica dining room table Dad made at the Shop; the big, golden whirly-burl coffee table they finished together; china cabinet and china; her small organ; a rocking chair; things that held meaning for her. She left the rest of her household goods for the auction and took her truck full of belongings to a storage unit in Seattle. Her glass canning jars filled with peaches, pears, tomatoes, string beans, and applesauce; the frozen corn, rhubarb, raspberries, and strawberries—all the colorful jewels of her homemaking—she took to Robin's house, where she stayed while Dad awaited testing.

The auctioneer Mom hired took Dad's Airstream trailer in partial payment for auctioning off their thirty-seven-year accumulation of belongings. He was a good man, practical and kind. He and his crew cataloged carpentry tools from the tool shed, Pop's antique chisels and hand planes, the sweet-smelling leather harnesses, and Pop's precious grinding wheel. The staff went through the barn full of dusty farm equipment, and... the stuffed outbuildings scattered with cobwebs and dead flies. They found stored furniture, Nana's hope chest, which I kept, tables, lamps, and chairs. They discovered the unused generator and large stash of emergency food rations Dad bought in 1972. There was so much to look through it took six people three weeks to organize. The auction was set for mid-October. With her destiny uncertain, Mom had left most of her household furniture to be sold. She needed as much money as possible from the auction to pay for Dad's future care.

I was sad to see the farm go, but mostly for Mom and Dad, not for me. I had sweet memories of a multitude of visits over the years as our children grew up enjoying the magic of their grandparent's life. They had all ridden the tractor and mopeds and swum in Dad's pool made from a large, circular, galvanized-zinc cattle watering tank. They had been there each Labor Day for the Ellensburg Rodeo, ice skated on a frozen pond, slept on the sleeping porch, made apple cider, and consumed oodles of Grandma Pauline's desserts. Grandma and Grandpa's goodness would live on in grateful hearts.

Auction day arrived, a sunny, mild, October Saturday, perfect for a big crowd. People came from everywhere; cars parked up and down the road. Bidding was brisk as boxes full of miscellaneous items were sold first, to curious bidders hoping for a valuable surprise. Mom stayed in Seattle to be with Dad, but also, I think she couldn't bear watching her life being sold. She told Dad about the auction but I'm not sure it registered. Alice, Morrie, and I were there to see the bidding and sales; we all found it hard to watch possessions go. Mom had a spare, black, old-fashioned baby doll from her childhood that was a treasure. I foolishly let it go, thinking it would bring a high value. It didn't. While I wasn't looking, Morrie bought Pop's old wooden toolbox with his tools, and Carol's cross-country skis, wetsuit, and water ski—memories of Pop and Carol.

The auctioneer's stuttering chatter flew by, urging the bargainers to out-bid each other. After the mystery boxes came tools and assortments of household items, pots and pans, mixers, and canning supplies, then the furniture. The larger, most expensive farm equipment was saved for the afternoon. Throughout the morning the bidding was hot and the selling fast, great for Mom's finances.

Around noon, a deputy sheriff approached the auctioneer and quietly told him that the auction would be shut down if the cars parked along the county road were not moved. The neighbor across the street, who bought the house and one acre from Dad, had called the sheriff because cars were parked on his property. Many bidders left to move their cars and then went home. With customers lost, the furious pace of the auction slowed as the remaining morning lots were sold. Farm equipment, Dad's tractor, plow, mower, tedder, hay baler, his Troy-Bilt rototiller, and a roomful of packaged survival food were among the items on the block that afternoon, but because of the interruption, rhythm slacked. With a lack of bidders, the bids were lower, and the more expensive items sold for less. Mom lost desperate dollars.

Karma shows no mercy. Sadly, within the next year,

the neighbor and his wife were killed when their car drove under a semi on the freeway.

The auction over, Alice, Morrie, and I registered at a motel, exhausted by the emotion of the day. We shared a room to save money, and as we were falling asleep heard a thump on the wall between rooms, then another, and another. As the thumps sped up, we realized their significance and sputtered in the dark with embarrassed amusement—the circle of life.

The sky was high and blue the next morning when we left Ellensburg. It had been a successful, though stomach-wrenching, weekend and as we traveled back over Snoqualmie Pass, a pickup truck went by carrying the farm's outhouse in the back, the door flapping a fond farewell.

We understood having to sell the farm. Mom would need somewhere to live with or without Dad. Alice found a lot north of Seattle, in Mill Creek, near Robin and herself. With a construction loan, Mom, Alice, and Robin began to plan a new house. They decided not to tell Dad yet, and between visits to his facility found a builder and approved a design. Mom made the decisions while Alice and Robin took care of the building process. It wouldn't be ready until spring, but there were a lot of bridges for Dad to cross before then.

CHAPTER TWENTY-SIX
Resolution
October 1995

As we drove through the busy morning streets, windshield wipers slapping side to side, black and orange Halloween decorations, red and yellow autumn leaves, and glaring headlights blurred together through our rain-splattered windows like a Monet painting. The day of Dad's appointment had finally arrived. He sat placidly, his face relaxed, his resolve for vindication holding back fear. I sat wishing for a miracle to bring back my real Dad. Though he seemed calm, he was floundering. His medications helped but waiting for his appointment with the University of Washington doctors was unnerving. Throughout this ordeal he'd felt mistreated and undermined, unable to help himself, a leaf caught in an eddy, headed for the storm drain. If he didn't ace this next examination he would lose everything.

The quaint red-brick building, in a university district neighborhood, was unlike the streamlined medical facility I expected. Gripping our dripping umbrellas, Mom, Dad, and I, slogged through the wet maple leaves toward the clinic door that opened automatically into a warm, bright lobby. We registered and waited.

The University of Washington's Alzheimer's Disease Research Center, ADRC, was established in 1885. Now, one hundred and ten years later, Alzheimer's is still a mystery, autopsy being the only option for an accurate diagnosis. Dad's was another study still trying to unlock the mystery of Alzheimer's disease.

Dad was scheduled for a complete assessment considering all causes. By mid-morning, he was busy with the first of his tests which would continue for three days: clinical interview, verbal comprehension test, perceptual reasoning test, working memory test, processing speed test, personality assessment, behavioral assessment. Some were simple like naming the current president, today's date, and year; remembering three words after drawing the face of a clock; repeating a series of numbers; copying a simple box-like drawing. Then there were the deeper psychological evaluations. The tests were continual. Dad went back to the Alzheimer's home in the evening and was back early each morning for more. Exhausting. Thorough. Dad/John's yearning to get back to the farm kept him working hard to finish each test. He didn't realize his abilities were minimal. When we were growing up, Dad told us our minds were like pigeonholes, small compartments in an old-fashioned post office, and we should keep them filled with good things. Throughout his life, he'd worked earnestly at that. Now his pigeonholes were empty.

When the tests were done, Dad returned to his temporary home to wait for answers. By now, waiting was second nature. Over the last year, we'd spent long stretches of uncertainty between short bursts of terror as life went on. While we faced the chaos of Dad's altering personality, Windows 95 came out, Yahoo started up, "Toy Story" was released, and OJ Simpson was acquitted. Patience accompanied our drama.

The day the assessment was ready, the family gathered to hear the diagnosis. We learned Dad's problem was not Alzheimer's, but Multi-infarct-dementia or MID. Multi-infarct-dementia is a vascular disease caused by multiple mini-strokes—infarcts—in the brain. Clots in small vessels cause brain tissue to die from lack of oxygen. These mini-strokes damaged Dad's brain tissue in several specific areas, most noticeably in the region controlling his paranoia. This allowed his bizarre behavior to run unrestrained and lead him to the legal system.

The best news was, Dad could live at home with new medications. That approval was like feeling sand beneath your feet after being lost at sea. The long, frenzied months of life-changing events had ended in Dad's deliverance. I was especially thankful that the University of Washington's study had saved Dad from living in the brown and yellow nursing home in Ellensburg for the rest of his life.

However, one problem remained—taking Dad's car keys away. We were cowards. Driving was his life, his freedom, and power. However, over the last few years, he had shrunk—he was only five feet, seven inches to begin with—and now sat so low in the driver's seat of the big Suburban, when he drove he looked like "Where's Waldo" peeking over the steering wheel. Hoping Mom would supervise his driving, we ignored the responsibility. Because he had also had a stroke, the doctors agreed to help us and alert the State Patrol to have Dad's license revoked to save us from confronting him.

With the approval of the University of Washington medical team, Dad was free to leave the nursing home. The judge signed his release. Our relief was profound. But would we get John or Dad?

With that in mind, Mom and Dad came to live with us on Fox Island. Our attached cottage gave them privacy, but we could still watch over them. It had a bedroom, bathroom with walk-in shower, and a combined kitchen and living room with a cozy fireplace.

It turned out we got Dan, mostly Dad but with a little John, though he was so medicated he seemed dormant much of the time, with a slow shuffle and often a vacant stare. On good days he was Dad, happy to be with his family, and able to putter at small carpentry projects that made him feel useful, or spend time in the yard, enjoying the fresh air. They settled in attending a church on the island and Mom adopted the neighborhood. She bathed, fed, and cared for Dad in the little cottage, and baked goodies for friends and neighbors in her small kitchen. Both made the best of their new surroundings.

When Christmas Day came, the air was crisp, cheeks were pink, and frozen pine needles crackled underfoot. Our house was warm and scented with spiced cider when families arrived with presents for under the tree. We opened gifts after the big dinner and dessert, happy to be together, and grateful Dad was with us. He enjoyed being surrounded by his loved ones and smiled at his grandchildren's happy faces as the gift wrappings were ripped. More dessert and more visiting until it was time to leave. Long goodbyes and waving as the last car went down the lane. A most wonderful day.

"Good morning," I said as Mom and Dad walked in the front door the next day. "Can I get you a cup of tea, Mom? Coffee, Dad?"

Morrie came into the kitchen humming "*O Come, All Ye Faithful*." We all sat at the kitchen counter, laughing about yesterday's fun.

"It was nice to see all the nieces and nephews," Morrie said. "They're growing up so fast."

"They seemed happy with their presents." I smiled at Mom. "And Anika was tickled with the coat you and Dad gave her."

"The dinner was a big success." Mom sipped her tea. "Cooking the turkey in a bag made it so moist. I'll have to try it for Easter."

As we talked, Dad looked more and more confused. "Was Christmas yesterday?" he asked. We nodded. "I lost Christmas," he whispered and bowed his head in despair. The drugs had wiped Christmas from his memory.

During the winter months, Mom joined the health club where our daughter Anika worked. Doing water aerobics helped with her arthritis and gave her time for herself. While she was in her class, Dad and I walked the indoor track. He loved to walk and knew it was good for him, which he proved every time we went. He'd go from dormant to counting to ten in Spanish as the rhythmic movement stirred blood to his brain and his morale always increased a bit.

Over the winter, the house in Mill Creek took shape. My sisters, talented designers, gave it their best. Because Fox Island was so quiet with our children grown, Mom, the fountain of energy, was looking forward to moving north of Seattle near Alice and Robin where she could help with her younger grandchildren. She'd lived in Edmonds during the 1940s and 1950s and was happy to be coming back to the area with Dad.

The winter passed and the daffodils were blooming for Dad's 84th birthday on March 12. Foolishly, Mom must have shown him his driver's license renewal notice. Instead of telling him his driving days were over, she agreed to drive him to the licensing office the next day. I think she found it impossible to separate Bob of the past from Bob-John of the present.

When I heard the plan, I realized the University of Washington doctors had never alerted the authorities. Mom was helpless; I'd have to deal with the problem. In anguish, I called the State Patrol office. I filled out the paperwork they faxed and sent it back just before the office closed. Of everything I had to do during Dad's illness, taking away his freedom to drive was the worst.

When he reached the licensing office the next morning, Dad walked up to the counter when it was his turn. "My name is Robert Davison and I'm here to renew my driver's license," Dad said, handing in his old one. The man at the counter looked at his license, then some paperwork. "I'm sorry Mr. Davison, but your license has been revoked."

Of course, Dad was crushed. He hadn't expected denial. Head drooped and shoulders slumped, he stood there until Mom led him away. For him, the last vestige of his manhood had been taken away. He wouldn't be able to hurt anyone, but it felt like I'd closed his coffin lid.

CHAPTER TWENTY-SEVEN
The End
January 1996—August 1996

Mom's house in Mill Creek sprang from the ground like spring crocuses. Only a five-minute drive from Robin's home, it was lovely and small, in a new community, with walking trails for Dad. Planning through the winter had given Mom time for a few short trips to the worksite north of Seattle, and to figure out details with Alice over the phone. When Mom was with Alice, Dad was with us or a caretaker from Catholic Community Services.

To keep him from worrying, the new house was kept a secret until it was almost done. Mom surprised him with the happy news at the end of March. He was furious.

"I thought we had no money," he yelled. "You've tricked me!" His eyes squinted meanness and his fists clenched with anger. "You've been lying all along while sneaking behind my back to steal my money and make a fool of me."

The obstacle course of Mom's life gave her another

THWACK! John was back.

It dawned on me then, that Dad had considered the farm auction a foreclosure—a family bankrupted—the bank selling off belongings. He had seen these during the Great Depression. Ever since the auction last October he thought they were penniless, poverty-stricken. Painful for Mom to discover he had misunderstood, she quietly explained their finances, he calmed down, and after lunch, he began to ask about the new house.

By April, Alice and Robin had finished decorating, had retrieved belongings from the storage facility, and with everything in place, Mom and Dad moved from the tiny cottage into their new home. When Dad walked through the front door for the first time, he saw an open, high-ceilinged living room and kitchen, granite countertops, a master bedroom with adjoining bathroom and step–in shower, a guest bedroom, office, and garage—spic-and-span, brand new. Happy to be on their own again, they quickly settled in. Mom continued taking good care of him but in loyalty, overlooked the signs of his failing. Under terrible stress, not wanting to feel, Mom became a *doing*, not a *being*. She kept herself too busy to think.

Over the summer, they joined Robin's church, spent time going for car rides, working on the small garden in the backyard, and happily being near Alice's and Robin's young families. Things seemed to go along smoothly.

However, Mom was unaware that one of the last stages of dying was the inability to swallow. She hadn't read the Alzheimer's information so she was determined to make Dad eat his nutritious chicken dinners, ignorant of the fact that he couldn't. When he tried and failed, she became frustrated. By August, Dad was nearing the end of his life. Was Mom aware? I don't know. She just kept her busy routine.

This put our daughter Amie in a predicament. Five months pregnant, she drove from Seattle to take her grandpa for a gentle walk in the new neighborhood. He'd always loved to walk.

Still refusing to admit Dad's frail condition, Mom didn't mention that he hadn't been eating; she was determined that he would. As Amie waited, Mom helped him into his coat and happily sent them out the door. They hadn't gone far when Dad's weakness took over; he couldn't go any farther. In a quandary, Amie left him sitting on a curb, hurried back for her car, and brought him back to Mom. On her way home she was shaken by the depth of Grandma's denial.

The end came a few days later and providence led me there. Ours is a musical family, dealing in everything from live performance to the recording industry. On August 6, Morrie, our daughter Jennifer, and I had a vocal session on Camano Island, north of Mom and Dad's new house. The recording equipment broke down and we left early to visit them.

When we walked in the door, Dad lay in a recliner, in the living room, asleep—his snoring was strong and loud; I didn't know it was the "death rattle"—a sound likened to a coffee percolator. Hospice had sent a nurse the night before to give Mom some rest, and Dad had fallen into a coma sometime during the early morning hours. The nurse left, my sisters came, and Mom, on autopilot, made breakfast.

We recognized this was a serious time and surrounded

Dad with our chatter, anesthetizing ourselves with talk as he slept in the plush turquoise recliner, snoring his loud, percolating snore.

At some point, our voices were shouting over the snoring, so we managed to get Dad into the nearby bedroom and tuck him into bed. We thought we had more time. How naive we were. Not knowing how to help Mom, other than being with her, we continued to visit in the living room without comprehending Dad lay dying in the bedroom. We seemed to have mass paralysis at this deeply spiritual moment. Mom was numb and her timing was off. She was preparing food in the open kitchen when she would rather have been at Dad's bedside holding his hand.

I recall times in my life when I was dozing, feeling completely safe and content, warm and cozy, listening to my family's voices coming from somewhere nearby. I like to imagine that is how Dad felt as he listened to the beloved sounds coming from the living room. Dear voices of the precious family he'd worked so hard to give a good life.

Morrie understood our stress better than we did, and as we worked on lunch in the kitchen, he stepped into his father-in-law's bedroom to check on him. Morrie rested his hand on Dad's hand. In a few moments, Dad's body sagged, and he slipped away.

Quietly, Morrie brought us the news. Mom sat with Dad while the coroner was called. I phoned my family, and Alice and Robin contacted theirs. Before the business of death began, Robin put her three-year-old daughter, Emily, down for a nap. Then we waited through the official part of a home death.

Later, when Dad's body was gone with the funeral

directors and coroner, Emily woke up from her nap. "Where's Grandpa?" she asked Mom.

"He's gone to heaven," Mom answered.

"Nuh-uh," she protested.

"Go look in his room," Grandma said.

Emily went and stood in the doorway of the empty room where she had last seen him, then returned to the living room, a sweet and true believer.

The sky cried at his graveside service and umbrellas sprang open. There was not enough room under the canopied shelter to cover all the family and friends who came. Songs were sung and comforting words were spoken. His journey over, he could rest in peace, having done his best. My sweet dad. What a wonderful life he had given us, full of adventures and happy memories. A humble man who throughout his life followed the teachings of a lowly carpenter and whose simplicity of spirit desired only a wooden box for a resting place. Beautiful long, smooth, pine boards, light saffron and cream, striated with golden streaks, and, like life, a sprinkle of knots, honored his journey.

His ancestors awaited him in the family plot he'd thought to buy so many years ago. On a slight, grassy hillside, where sun brightened the vista of trees, stone markers, and green carpet beyond, he'd join his mama, Ivy; father, Pop; and sisters, Queenie, Letha, Phyllis, and Christel, with a space saved beside him for his sweetheart Pauline.

His skiff "Dementia" tied to a dock on the invisible river, worries gone, he was welcomed by Carol, Pop, Nana and his siblings, in the happiest of places.

EPILOGUE

1997—2011

Mom was 78 when Dad died. The short time they lived in the little house together christened it with sweet memories for her to hold when he was gone. After a year, her travel bug began to itch, and since she'd only traveled in the United States, she decided it was time to see the rest of the world. She planned a chock-full trip to New Zealand and Australia with Alice, Robin and me along to give her courage. We began with a flight to one of the beautiful islands of Fiji, then flew to Auckland, New Zealand. After Mom graciously declined an offer for a free jump at Auckland's Greenhithe Bridge, where bungee jumping began, we continued on to Franz Josef Glacier, Milford Sound, and Christchurch. In Rotorua we rubbed noses in greeting, then dined in a Wharenui (Wer-en-you-ee), a Maori communal center, and the next day visited Maori thermal pools where grave mounds were placed above the heated ground. Better than that, though, was watching Mom, in front of me, racing down the mountainside-track in a pseudo-luge go-kart, with a big smile on her 80-year-old face.

In Australia we did as much as possible, from hot-air ballooning with kangaroos jumping below, to boomerang throwing at Tjapukai (Ja-poo-kii) Aboriginal Cultural Park. Mom donned her swimsuit to snorkel on the Great Barrier Reef, bussed through the outback to Alice Springs, watched us climb the sacred rock, Uluru, and boated through the Crocodile Dundee country of Darwin. The trip was a marathon of wonder, whetting Mom's palate for more international travel.

For the next eight years she traveled. She visited Russia with Robin's church, spent a Fourth of July on Israel's Sea of Galilee, took in Egypt, China, and Germany. She took a cruise to France, Italy, Ireland, and England, another to Columbia, the Panama Canal, Costa Rica, and Mexico. She visited Belize and Honduras on a Caribbean trip, and Italy, Minorca, Malta, and Spain in the Mediterranean. In China, her group went to a knockoff North Face factory, which she thought was the real thing. She bought fifteen different jackets for Christmas presents that necessitated fellow AAA travelers helping her take some through customs. Sweet, generous, frugal Mom was unaware of the drama she caused. After that, Alice, Robin, or I accompanied her whenever she traveled.

She and I had a wonderful time in Paris with cousins who lived in Germany. We stayed in a Parisian flat and shopped at the outdoor markets, bought bread, Brie, and wine, viewed the Mona Lisa at the Louvre, and climbed the Eiffel Tower. With Mom, traveling was always fun.

When she was 87, she had been to every continent in the world but one—Antarctica. It was not to be left undone.

In 2005, Mom, Alice and I took a cruise to South

America with Antarctica in mind. We started in Argentina with its gauchos, sizzling steaks and top-quality leather. Then on to Uruguay, the Falkland Islands, and stopped at the bottom of the world, Ushuaia, Argentina. From there we boarded a bus to nearby Punta Arenas, Chili, where a plane would fly us to the Chilean station in Antarctica. However, there was a problem. As we waited on our buses at the airport to board the plane, the tour guide called me outside.

"Your mom can't go with us," Maria, the guide in charge of our tour said. "There will be a lot of walking and no place for your mom to stay at the station."

I knew Mom couldn't walk far, even with her cane, because of her arthritic back. But no way was I giving up.

"My sister and I will help her walk. We can support her on either side. This is so significant for her. The only continent she hasn't traveled. She'll be crushed if she can't go."

"I'm sorry," Maria offered, "but the tour is vigorous. She'll have to get in and out of an inflated boat for a trip to a penguin sanctuary, and the rest of the tour involves a lot of walking. If it's too hard for her, there is no place for her to wait."

"This is really important to her," I said. "She's been excited about going there for months. She's 87, and so close to her goal."

Our conversation went back and forth for a few minutes. Finally, I said, "Okay. But I can't tell her. You'll have to tell her."

Maria couldn't tell her either, and let Mom go on the trip. Mom waited for us in the cozy lounge of the Chilean

Station Hotel where the scientists stay. Alice and I saw the penguins and took the tour. With great satisfaction, Mom completed the trip to her last continent.

Pauline Theda Davison, 87

A "good and faithful servant," she lived free of the illness Dad had. Still driving, she relished life, church, and Costco for the next six years, happily living with Robin's family, in her own private suite, with a sweeping view of Puget Sound.

At almost 93, she joined Dad on the grassy knoll, in April of 2011.

The end of an era.

Pauli Pedersen and her husband live on Fox Island in Washington State. Between the majestic Olympic mountain range to the west and Mount Rainier to the east they are surrounded by waters of the Puget Sound, and visited occasionally by deer under the apple tree, a racoon on the prowl, or an eagle gliding over nearby Honeymoon Bay.

    An active life of teaching, raising five charming children, and performing as a classical singer gave way to the opportunity to indulge her love of words. With a Bachelor of Arts Degree in English and an indefatigable spirit, she finds wonder in her family history.